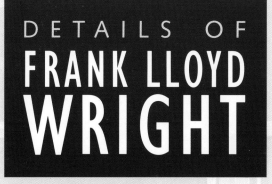

DETAILS OF
# FRANK LLOYD
# WRIGHT

# Details of Frank Lloyd Wright

## The California Work, 1909-1974

Thames and Hudson

Photographs by **Scot Zimmerman**

Text by **Judith Dunham**

Introduction by **Eric Lloyd Wright**

## Acknowledgments

We are very grateful to all of the owners and caretakers of Frank Lloyd Wright's buildings in California, who shared with us the history of the buildings and generously allowed photographs of them.

We also thank Eric Lloyd Wright, Arthur Dyson, Al Strukus, Steve Fernandez, Jeffrey Chusid, Barbara Ashbaugh, Robert Ooley, Joe Fabris, Aaron Green, and Robert Beharka for their invaluable assistance with research and logistics.

*—Judith Dunham and Scot Zimmerman*

First published in Great Britain in 1994 by
Thames and Hudson Ltd, London

First published in the USA in 1994 by
Chronicle Books, 275 Fifth Street, San Francisco, CA 94103

Photographs copyright © 1994 by Scot Zimmerman
Text copyright © 1994 by Judith Dunham
Introduction copyright © 1994 by Eric Lloyd Wright

British Library Cataloguing-in-Publication Data

A catalogue record for this book is available from the British Library

ISBN 0-500-34134-6

Printed and bound in Hong Kong

# CONTENTS

Introduction
by Eric Lloyd
Wright

6

1909
Stewart Residence

22

1917
Barnsdall
Residence

26

1923
Millard Residence

36

1923
Ennis-Brown
Residence

40

1923
Storer Residence

48

1923
Freeman Residence

56

1936
Hanna Residence

62

1939
Bazett-Frank
Residence

66

1939
Sturges Residence

72

1940–41
Oboler Gatehouse
and Studio-Retreat

76

1948
Walker Residence

80

1948
Buehler Residence

84

1948
Morris Gift Shop

90

1950
Berger Residence

96

1950
Mathews Residence

102

1950
Pearce Residence

104

1952
Anderton Court
Shops

108

1955
Kundert Medical
Clinic

112

1955
Fawcett Residence

116

1957
Walton Residence

120

1957
Marin County
Civic Center

124

1958
Ablin Residence

132

1958
Pilgrim
Congregational
Church

136

1974
Bell-Feldman
Residence

140

Further Reading

144

# I N T R O D U C T I O N

Eric Lloyd Wright

**D**etails are essential to the creation of a great work of architecture. It is true that Louis Sullivan, Frank Lloyd Wright's mentor, used to say "from generals to particulars." Once the generals were laid out, the particulars came into play, and those who have seen Sullivan's work know that he was particular about the "particulars." Wright was also particular about details. Most of us think of Wright as producing simplicity in architecture. A closer examination of his buildings—an examination that inevitably focuses on the details—reveals that they were probably some of the most complex buildings in the twentieth century. They were complex but never complicated. It was his genius to create a simple whole out of a complexity of parts.

I can remember Sunday breakfasts at Taliesin when my grandfather would talk to the Fellowship about philosophy and architecture. One Sunday morning he had on the table beside him a group of shells, conchs, turbans, clams, pectens, cowries, murexes, and volutes. He pointed to the shells and told us to observe how this one germ idea for housing a creature in the ocean could take so many shapes. He noted the intricate fluting and sculptured patterns on different shells, the wide range of colors and designs, and how no two shells even of the same subspecies were identical. He went on to talk about the complexity of an oak tree. Its small flowers made up of petals and stamens attached to small branches having leaves of an articulated shape. There being literally thousands of leaves and flowers attached to the small branches, which are attached to larger branches, which are attached to the trunk. The branches and trunk covered with bark of variegated patterns. The trunk going into the ground and becoming roots. All of this complexity making up the simple silhouette of

▶ Colonnade,
Ennis-Brown residence,
Los Angeles.

the oak tree, just as the complexity of the seashell makes up a simple, basic form. "This," he said, "is the model you should use in developing your buildings. Nature will show you the way to build."

Wright's concept of the designing of a building is that it grows from a germ idea like a plant growing from a seed. In the seed is the genetic material that creates the form of the plant. So in Wright's work the seed was the floor plan. The unit system he chose for his plans became the "cells" of the building, which were multiplied both vertically and horizontally, the combination of various cells forming the different spaces and details. But all of these spaces and details were related to the original germ idea and were reflected in the unit system. In the early part of his practice, most of the unit systems were square, seen in the right-angle designs of the windows, doors, and walls, and of the furniture and fixtures. As he progressed, Wright began working with forty-five-degree and thirty-degree unit systems and in later schemes with circles and ellipses. Whatever form he selected to express the nature of a building, it was the unit system that held the form together and created the rhythm of the building, and helped keep the proportion of the building, in plan, elevation, and details. The details were an organic outgrowth of the unit system, and if their relationship to the system did not appear direct, they would always have a connection to the spirit of the space.

Wright was concerned with the creation of space, the space within the physical form. He was fond of quoting the great Chinese philosopher Lao-tzu, who said, "The reality of the cup is not the cup itself but the space within the cup." When my grandfather read that as a young architect, he said

◄ Sawn-wood windows, Kundert Medical Clinic, San Luis Obispo.

to himself, "That is what I have been trying to do with my buildings. The reality of the building is the space within the building."

One of the most important elements in the creation of this space is the detailing, not only the architectural detailing, but the furnishings as well. Furniture, fixtures, and furnishings were built into the walls as much as possible to integrate them with the interior space by making a harmonious transition between floor and ceiling. While continually trying to simplify the space, he articulated these elements with designs that grew out of the unit system of the building and which thus helped establish interest, harmonious proportion, and human scale. Wright always worked with the idea of creating space that was proportioned for the human being. He sought to make the person in the building feel not small and insignificant but rather comfortable and in harmony with the space.

The details, through their relationship to the unit system, are a reflection of the larger spaces. This is very similar to the theory of fractals, where all parts, large and small, mirror the object as a whole and build on each other to create the whole. On first view, the space in a Wright building appears simple and uncluttered. You are allowed to absorb the basic feeling of the space. When you look closer, the articulation of the details makes itself evident so that no matter where you are in a room, you are aware of the immediate areas surrounding you, as well as of the total space.

Essential to Wright's concept of organic architecture is the integrated connection between exterior and interior. The exterior shell developed from the form of the interior space. Windows and doors were placed to form a movement, a continuum of space from inside to outside. There is no

▶ Living room, with Wright-designed furniture, Ablin residence, Bakersfield.

feeling of separation between them. He eliminated the post at the corner of a room and mitered the glass of the window. As soon as this was done, the "box" was broken open, and the interior space "flowed" out and became part of the outside. No longer bounded by the corner post, the inner space is released. Roof soffits pierce through the walls into the interior to become light shelves or the ceiling. Patterned concrete blocks or perforated wood boards give interesting light and shadow play to exterior walls. During the day, the pattern from the outside is created by looking through the glass at the interior shadow. From the inside, the pattern is created by looking through the glass to the light of the sky. The reverse happens at night, when the interior becomes lit and the outside dark. Both exterior and interior wall surfaces frequently are of the same material and patterns so that you feel the same sense of space as you pass from the outside to the inside. Roof trellis openings follow the interior unit system so that the rhythm of the exterior is in harmony with the interior. These various integrations of the details in harmony with the unit system helped Wright achieve the spirit of organic architecture.

From a distance you can sense the marvelous overall proportions of Wright's buildings. As you draw closer, the walls, roofs, and openings hold your attention. As you come upon the buildings, you are attracted to the wall patterns, or the light and shadow forms created by the trellis overhangs, or the patterned openings in the walls, or the ornamental roof fascia details. This ability of a building to hold your interest, from near and far, characterizes one of the elements of Wright's genius. Experienced up close, the details articulate the space, and because the details are integrated with

◄ Fountain at entrance
to Storer residence,
Hollywood.

the unit system and the structure, there is a unity that creates a sense of repose and strength.

A very important part of Wright's architecture is the way he integrated the structure of a building with finished surfaces through the detailing. He was concerned with the transition and terminal points of a structure, such as the meeting of floor and walls, the connection of walls to ceiling, and the transition from soffit to fascia to roof. His ability to unify all of these elements through the detailing gives his buildings a strong interrelationship of structure, surface, and openings, and therefore a distinctive character. One of the ways he did this was to use wood moldings over door heads and extend them around the room and over the windows to establish a strong horizontal line. He sometimes painted the area above the wood strip with a tint of the same color used below the strip. He used this color on the ceiling so that the areas of the wall above the molding seem to be part of the ceiling as well as part of the wall. In this way he created the illusion of the lack of a corner where the wall meets the ceiling. His approach to the floor was similar. If he was using an oak floor, he placed a wider than normal oak base against the wall, again illusionistically eliminating the corner between floor and wall, and developing a sense of continuous space.

Wright used light shelves to give the effect of a low ceiling, while allowing the main ceiling of a room to be high. This is especially effective in residences where you walk into a low-ceilinged entry hall from the main door and proceed around a corner to a living room, which has a high ceiling. This change in height from the entry to the living room gives a release and lift to the spirit. Usually the entry is placed so that you have only a glimpse of the living room as you enter the residence through the front door. The view is just enough to tantalize and entice you to move into the main room to discover the mystery around the corner.

Nature played a major role in the designs of Wright's buildings: the nature of the client, the society, the site, the geographical location, the materials, and the ability of the workmen. He created a grammar that was unique for some buildings. Other buildings, especially houses, used the same grammar because of the compatibility of use, site, and budget. The grammar was established by the floor plan and carried throughout the structure by the detailing. The parts were related to the whole as the whole to the parts. But the whole was always greater than the sum of the parts. It was the remarkable ability of Wright to maintain the grammar of the building in the details that allowed this synergy to happen. This was also the reason that he felt it was so important to design all the details, from windows to draperies, kitchen cabinets to dining chairs, light fixtures to door moldings. All were important to that creation of space.

"In Organic Architecture then," Wright wrote, "it is quite impossible to consider the building as one thing, its furnishings another and its setting and environment still another. The Spirit in which these buildings are conceived sees all these together at work as one thing. All are to be studiously foreseen and provided for in the nature of the structure. Incorporated (or excluded) are lighting, heating, and ventilation. The very chairs and tables, cabinets, and even musical instruments, where practicable, are of the building itself, never fixtures upon it. No appliances or fixtures are admitted as such where circumstances permit the full development of the organic character of the building scheme. Floor coverings and hangings are at least as much a part of the house as the plaster on the walls or the tiles on the roof."

If a building, he said, "is conceived in an organic sense, all ornamentation is conceived as of the very ground plan and is therefore of the very constitution of the structure itself." Ornament to Wright was an abstraction of nature. The ornamentation on plants and trees, with their trunks, stems, branches, leaves, and flowers, was a natural outgrowth of the structure and purpose of the plant. This integral relationship between ornament and structure was what Wright was striving to create.

The details of any art, especially those of the art of architecture, are critical in defining a piece of work and its meaning. Architecture is a three-dimensional art form, and the details help define and articulate the sense of scale. They create and emphasize light and shadow, modulate the transitions between vertical and horizontal planes, and create a rhythm that can give an underlying "heartbeat" to a structure. The ability of detail to create rhythm adds a fourth dimension to building, that of depth, not physical depth, but a depth of soul and spirit.

Throughout the history of humankind, architects, designers, and craftspeople have been intrigued with the details. In making an ax, it was not enough just to tie a chipped stone to a wood handle. The true artisan took care in shaping the stone head, and was concerned about how neatly the leather thongs held the stone head to the wood handle and how the tying of the thong created a beautiful pattern in itself. The handle might be carved with a design that helped to grip the ax and

◀ Wall of glass-filled, perforated concrete blocks, Ablin residence, Bakersfield.

also added to the physical beauty. The Anasazi enhanced the beauty of their pots by the strong, simple, stylized images they painted on them. The Mayans created a feeling of strength and awe with the repeated friezes they carved on their buildings. The bold patterns on the bronze vases of early Chinese cultures also showed this need for detail.

The tepee of the Plains Indians was a piece of organic architecture. Its twenty-eight poles reflected a unit system conforming to the twenty-eight days of the cycle of the moon. The hole in the center not only let smoke out but let light in. The smoke flaps that controlled the wind entering the smoke outlet were beautiful as well as functional. The exterior skins of the tepee were painted mainly with different abstract geometric patterns or sometimes with animals and hunting scenes. The interior had a tent liner of leather and a floor covered with buffalo robes. Shields and weapons were hung in a way that added to the overall sense of beauty and order. In these and other great cultures, we see an attention to detail to create a beautiful piece of craftsmanship or to create a beautiful space in which to live.

One measurement of the quality of a culture is how well it handles the details. Wright was fond of quoting a Frenchman who said, "The United States is the only civilization to go from barbarism to degeneracy with no culture in between." Yet as you view the various buildings in this book, you can see that the United States does have a culture of its own, and Wright, the free-thinking, democratic individual in tune with nature, was able to take that culture and express it in architecture. The photographs in this book, representing twenty-four buildings in California, offer a great

diversity of forms. In all these forms there is a unifying spirit that makes them recognizable as the work of Frank Lloyd Wright. One of the keys to this unifying spirit is his handling of the details.

From the Stewart residence of 1909 to the Pilgrim Congregational Church of 1958, this unity is evident in diversity. The plans of the buildings range from squares to thirty-degree and sixty-degree parallelograms, to hexagons, to circular and elliptical forms. The buildings include residences, a civic center, a medical clinic, a church, and two stores. The materials used are wood, stone, concrete, brick, concrete block, steel, and wood frame with wood and stucco facings. Many of the houses, such as the 1948 Walker residence in Carmel, were designed from basic plans to be built throughout the country, with special adaptations for specific sites. Other buildings, such as the textile-block houses in Los Angeles, were designed especially for the southern California landscape. The California buildings represent a full range of Wright's expression. Each is his unique statement, in organic terms, about the architect, owner, site, and society.

Scot Zimmerman, by way of his insightful photographs, and Judith Dunham, with her thoughtful text, have brought together an important part of Frank Lloyd Wright's concept of architecture, the details. It is hoped that, by seeing the pictures and reading the text, the reader will be motivated to seek out the buildings of Wright and, if they are open to the public, actually experience their spaces. The space within—that is the ultimate expression of Wright's architecture. It is the details that help create and articulate this space.

# STEWART RESIDENCE
### 1 9 0 9 • M o n t e c i t o

In commissions that are ranked among his most important works, Wright had already evolved and richly expressed his ideas for the Prairie house when he designed a residence for George C. and Emily Stewart, his first completed project in California. Stewart, an accountant, had immigrated to California from Scotland. Upon settling in Fresno, he met his future wife, Emily, also Scottish, who had resided in New York before coming west. After their marriage, in 1906, the Stewarts remained in Fresno, living on their large farm, where they maintained a vineyard and orchards. Shortly after they were married, they chose Montecito, then a rural town, as the location for a vacation home. Wright's work may have come to the Stewarts' attention through design magazines they acquired in San Francisco, where they had a second residence, since it is unlikely that they saw the architect's Prairie residences firsthand.

Faced with a notably different climate and landscape than found in the Midwest, Wright effectively transplanted salient elements of his Prairie "grammar" to this new environment and shaped them into a house that befits its verdant coastal surroundings north of Los Angeles. The broad planes and deep overhangs of the roof ground the two-story structure to its site. As Wright used masonry to further emphasize the horizontality of his Prairie houses, here he employs redwood board and batten, a practical and esthetic choice of a West Coast material. On his plans Wright labeled the house a "summer cottage." Though it is much larger than the description connotes—the floor area

▲ Stewart house, viewed from the north. The main entrance is to the left of the wing in the foreground, under the second-level balcony. This wing was originally a dining room. When the kitchen was moved to the rear of the house in the 1930s, the corresponding space on the south side, originally a porch, became the dining room.

◄ The living room is a soaring space surrounded on three sides by windows. Around the wall to the right of the fireplace is the staircase to the second floor. The two windows above the mantel extension provide a view onto the living room from the stairs. Another vantage can be gained from the balcony above the fireplace. The oak ceiling trim conforms to the grid of the plan and unites the ceiling with the rest of the room.

▼ The oak mantel continues across the living-room wall to form a shelf emphasizing the horizontal lines of Wright's plan. In contrast to the rectilinearity of the room, the inner wall of the fireplace is a semicircle. The oak floors are original and restored.

▲ Trellises extend from the
windows on the north side of
the living room. Shadows
created by the sunlight falling
across the redwood board
and batten highlight their
horizontal lines.

is forty-five hundred square feet—its setting and acknowledgment of the region's moderate climate convey its purpose as a country home. The site, now one acre, was originally five acres and also included stables, which were later converted into a house and sold. A two-bedroom guesthouse is still on the property. The second floor has sun porches that in warm weather could be used as sleeping porches.

Because of the darkness of the exterior and the surrounding foliage, it is difficult to sense, when approaching the facade, the light, airy quality of the interior. The full impact of the living room, the largest room in the house, is felt immediately upon stepping over the threshold into the two-story space, which surrounds one with windows that strive to re-create the feeling of being outdoors. The living-room fireplace is within the masonry core that forms the center of the cruciform plan. Projecting over the fireplace is a second-floor balcony that helps to define within the large room a more intimate area around the hearth. Reached by stairs behind the hearth, the balcony offers a view out the east wall of windows into the tangle of foliage and also accesses the bedrooms on the north, west, and south arms of the cruciform.

Wright's treatment of detailing elsewhere in the residence is modest and understated, in keeping with the intent of the house as a country home. As he would continue to do in many of his buildings in California and elsewhere, he provided areas for outdoor planting—trellises and terraces—which are also formal elements important to the overall design. Here at the Stewart house, Wright paid particular attention to the windows—there are 365 of them—that wrap around the house. Whereas he often used art glass in his Prairie residences, these windows as well as the interior glass doors have redwood mullions. They transform these transparent surfaces into simple yet elegantly proportioned compositions that manipulate light and shadow, taking full advantage of natural light during the day and artificial light at night.

◄ Opposite the living-room fireplace is an alcove of windows that faces east. The geometric patterns of the mullions are repeated, with variations, in the doors and built-in cabinetry elsewhere in the house. In the original house, all the interior windowsills and door and window frames were probably redwood—Wright's way of harmonizing interior and exterior. The lights, though not designed by Wright, date to the early 1900s.

▼ Unusually wide French doors—each nearly four feet wide—and screened openings separate the living room, in the foreground, and the front room. The main entrance is to the right. Around the corner to the left are the stairs to the second floor. The only piece of furniture Wright designed for the house is a cabinet built into an alcove in the north wall of the front room.

# BARNSDALL RESIDENCE

## 1917 • Hollywood

"No ordinary woman" was how Wright described Aline Barnsdall, a theater patron and sometime producer, who gave the architect his first major commission in California. Wright thought her planned arts community for thirty-six-acre Olive Hill in Los Angeles potentially "a generation or two ahead of itself." They embarked full of optimism on nearly ten years of work together, but an accumulation of delays and disagreements led to a rift between architect and client, and finally to the abandonment of the project. Of the several completed buildings, the grand house Wright designed for Barnsdall and her daughter is the only significant one that survives.

Design of the main house had yet to begin when Barnsdall decided to name it after her favorite flower, the hollyhock. Wright's abstract geometric rendering of the hollyhock, cast in concrete and used as integral ornamentation throughout the exterior and interior, comes into view as one ascends Olive Hill and arrives at the motor court on the north side of the house. Friezes of the motif relieve the massive parapets that press the building into the earth. This weightiness is accentuated by doors and windows—many of them employing art glass—seemingly recessed into the walls. Wright's evocation of pre-Columbian monumentality and imagery, which had already surfaced in his work, would reappear in the four textile-block houses that followed, where he took this sense of romance and mystery to even greater heights.

Not lacking in mystery itself, however, Hollyhock House guards its interior, especially from the over sixty-foot-long walkway leading from the motor court to the entry. The final several feet of this covered, walled path are

▲ Hollyhock House, viewed from the southwest. To the left is the west end of the living room, which looks out onto a reflecting pool. Beyond the wall to the right is the terrace outside the living room; rising above it is the parapeted roof of the library.

◀ Steps encircling the pool at the east end of the courtyard form an amphitheater facing back into the garden. Lloyd Wright, who supervised the early phases of the construction of the house, designed the landscaping, which included waterlilies and other plants in the pool. A pumping system pulled the water from this round pool into a stream along the north side of the garden and under the house to fill the pool in front of the fireplace and then the square pool outside the living room.

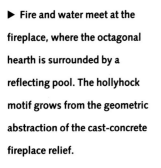 Fire and water meet at the fireplace, where the octagonal hearth is surrounded by a reflecting pool. The hollyhock motif grows from the geometric abstraction of the cast-concrete fireplace relief.

constricted by corbeled walls devoid of openings. At the end of this dark passage is a pair of cast concrete doors whose heft demands that they be opened slowly. After this choreographed experience, one can choose to head toward several living spaces, all of them visible from the entry.

The public spaces, opening to one another through wide doorways, wood screens, and art-glass windows, are uniquely defined in scale, elevation, and detail. The wood-paneled dining room, small for such a substantial house, is four steps above the level of the entry and music room, the living room one step below. Within the living room, the largest space in the house, the fireplace—its hearth surrounded by a reflecting pool and its wall bearing one of Wright's rare reliefs—is the focus. Wright designed two impressive sofas combined with tables, so that they could be set at an angle to the fireplace wall to create an enclave around the hearth and its pool. The palette of green and gold on the plaster ceiling is carried through the upholstery and carpet and in the Japanese screens placed in two corners as integral parts of the walls.

The living spaces and other rooms in the U-shaped plan look outward onto adjacent terraces, pools, and gardens, and, when possible, toward the city beyond Olive Hill. But the force that dominates is centripetal, pulling one through the loggia on the east side of the living room, or through the grand colonnade along the north wing of the house, into the inner garden courtyard. Although the courtyard opens to the east, a bridge connecting the north and south wings and their roof terraces preserves the sense of enclosure. Beneath the bridge is a circular pool whose amphitheater seating faces back into the garden and its shielding parapeted walls. Barnsdall's guests gathered here to view the theater productions she staged in the courtyard and on the roof terraces of the west wing. Today's visitors can also sit at the amphitheater to face the ever-present hollyhock icons watching over all.

▼ Two large sofas, each with attached desk and table, surround the fireplace to create a sitting area within the living room. Wright had previously combined pieces of furniture with different functions, but these, re-created from the oak originals, are particularly elaborate. The wide passageway at the left leads to the loggia off the foyer, which in turn opens onto the inner garden courtyard.

◄ Each desk, connected to a living-room sofa, has a torchiere whose support reiterates the hollyhock motif. The detailing along the side of the table is typical of Wright's preference for interlocking shapes, but the individual forms along the top of the sconce may have been added by R. M. Schindler, who did a number of drawings for the house. Through the doorway at the right is the music room, which is just inside the main entrance.

▲ The walls of the second-floor corridor follow the angle of the roof parapet.

◄ Wright's abstracted hollyhock pattern appears on the backs of the six dining-room chairs and on the base of the hexagonal table. The furniture and the walls are genesero, a hardwood from South America. The art-glass windows face north onto a small garden and the motor court. Four french doors on the opposite wall open on the colonnade along the inner garden court.

◀ Morning light filters through the trees and the geometric patterns of the art glass into the sleeping alcove. Wright designed the room for Barnsdall, though she rarely used it. Through the windows, it is possible to see the circular pool and amphitheater at the open end of the courtyard.

▲ Corbeled walls constrict the passageway to the front doors, which are concrete with narrow slits of glass. R. M. Schindler, who took over supervision of the construction after Lloyd Wright, made the drawings for the brass lock covers and may have designed them.

▶ Wright had planned to use concrete for Barnsdall's house, but for economic reasons he chose stucco over terra-cotta tile for the walls and stucco over wood frame for the roof parapets. He did cast in concrete the ornamental hollyhocks, which appear throughout the house as friezes, columns, colonnades, and planters.

◄ The playroom for
Barnsdall's daughter,
Betty, also known as
Sugar Top, projects from
the southwest corner of
the house, and its roof is
a balcony outside of her
mother's second-floor
bedroom, ornamented
with hollyhock finials.

▶ As Wright was to do
consistently in his later
work, he treats the
corners of Sugar Top's
playroom as transparent
planes that dissolve the
solid walls.

▶ For Aline Barnsdall's daughter, Wright designed a bedroom with an attached playroom, at the far left, surrounded on three sides by art-glass windows. The door to the left of the built-in bookshelves opens onto a small, child-size garden terrace. Lloyd Wright designed the desk. The chair is one of the elder Wright's.

▶ Art-glass windows and doors, like this window at the end of Sugar Top's playroom, have Wright's characteristic geometric motifs evoking the structure and growth of plants. The purple is the same color used in the panels appliquéd on the living-room drapery.

# MILLARD RESIDENCE

### 1923 • Pasadena

▲ Millard residence, viewed from the north. The main entrance is off the courtyard and under the bridge that connects the house, at left, and the garage, at right. The two bedrooms, placed above one another on the second and third floors, have narrow windows that look up the ravine on which the residence is sited.

The concrete block: Wright called it "that despised outcast" and the "cheapest (and ugliest) thing in the building world." Believing he could lift this outcast to a nobler plane, Wright set out to "educate" it. In the hands of its teacher, the block became the distinguishing feature of four stunning houses in southern California, beginning in 1923 with the one in Pasadena for Alice Millard.

Having commissioned a Prairie residence in Highland Park, Illinois, sixteen years earlier, Millard was receptive to Wright's concept for her new house, in a new location and climate, employing a new approach to concrete. The system he initiated at the Millard house he also applied, with modifications, to the other three southern California houses. The walls are actually made of an inner and outer block wall. Measuring sixteen inches square, the blocks have a patterned or a plain face and a coffered back. The exterior and interior blocks are separated by a one-inch airspace. A warp and weft of steel rods connects the blocks to one another, giving rise to the name "textile block" for Wright's method of construction.

The blocks, cast in a distinctive pattern that unified each house, often incorporated material excavated from the site, which gave them a porous, grainy texture. The Millard and the other houses required a variety of cast forms, depending on their functional and decorative use: plain and textured, solid and perforated, flat and angled at ninety degrees to fit corners. The references to weaving aptly describe not only the structure but also the

◀ Redwood-and-glass doors along the south wall of the living room open onto a narrow balcony and a view of the garden, pool, and studio. The perforated blocks in the wall above the doors create a screen of light.

▲ Millard residence, viewed from the south. The tall eucalyptus trees, the overgrown plantings, the irregular-shaped pool, and the topography of the site combine to enhance the romantic feeling of Wright's first textile-block house in California. The blocks, he wrote, are "textured like the trees." To the left of the main house is the studio Lloyd Wright added in 1926.

▶ The ceiling inside the entrance is under seven feet. The glass-paned doors and floor-to-ceiling windows bring natural light into what otherwise would be a dark, compressed space. The vertically stacked, perforated blocks are filled with glass.

▲ The main entry, a pair of redwood-framed glass doors, is on the second floor. Above the entrance is a bridge between the main house and the garage roof deck.

overall effect of the relief patterns when they are arranged into connected walls, volumes, columns, and walkways.

For Millard, Wright planned a residence he called La Miniatura, "the little studio-house," and was pleased that the fireproof concrete-block construction would protect her collection of books and other artworks. He assisted his client in the selection of the site, a ravine with eucalyptus trees that was bordered by streets to the north and south. In response to both location and climate, he created a three-story house that at every level opens onto terraces, balconies, and roof decks. Even the roof of the garage serves as a deck, joined to the house by a bridge that shades the main entrance. A separate studio, designed by Lloyd Wright and built in 1926, is also linked to the main house by a bridge between the studio roof and the living-room balcony.

The most dramatic interior feature of the Millard house is the two-story living room. As is characteristic of Wright's manipulation of space, the fifteen-foot-high living room opens up from the low-ceilinged entry, which is under seven feet. An interior balcony, reached from a staircase directly inside the entrance, overlooks the living room and provides the only access to the third-floor bedroom. Large areas of the walls are composed of unpatterned blocks, which provided plain surfaces for Millard to display her works of art. On the south wall of the living room, five glass doors flanked by narrow windows open out onto a balcony and a view of the garden and pool as well as of the studio. The area above these windows and doors is composed of perforated blocks that dapple the wall with light.

◀ The living-room fireplace is set underneath the third-floor balcony. To the right behind the fireplace are the stairs to the ground-floor dining room, kitchen, and servant's room.

▼ At both sides of the fireplace, setbacks using blocks cast at right angles create pleats of light and shadow.

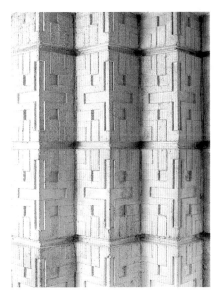

# ENNIS-BROWN RESIDENCE

## 1923 • Los Angeles

The Charles Ennis residence has long invited a rich array of allusions—to a Mayan temple, to a Persian palace, to a fortress of no specific origin. However deeply any of these references influenced Wright's formative concept for the house, they explain only some of the qualities that account for its forceful presence. Another is size: this is the largest of Wright's four textile-block residences. Still another is scale: the house is a two-story massing of forms buttressed structurally and visually by sizable retaining walls. Finally, there is location: the main house, courtyard, and garage with attached servant's quarters are laid out across a hill in the Los Feliz District of Los Angeles, where the complex can clearly be seen as one approaches it from below.

Inside the house, one feels separated from the world outside, despite the south-facing windows looking onto the city below. The rooms are few, but they are impressive in their majesty and formality. Underscoring the sense of grandeur is a one-hundred-foot-long colonnade that sweeps along the north side of the house and provides a transition from the public spaces to the two bedrooms. The colonnade, or loggia, begins at the west end of the second floor, where it is treated as an extension of the living spaces. From here, the rhythm of concrete-block columns beckons one to proceed east down the marble-tiled path.

The Ennis blocks, like those in the other textile-block houses, were cast with their own identifying design—an asymmetrical geometric abstraction—

▲ Ennis-Brown residence, viewed from the south.

▶ Seen in profile, from the west, the house steps out from the gated street entrance, at left. The covered entry into the courtyard also serves as a bridge between the garden terrace on the north side of the house and a smaller, more secluded garden northwest of the courtyard. The main entrance to the residence is underneath the second-floor overhang.

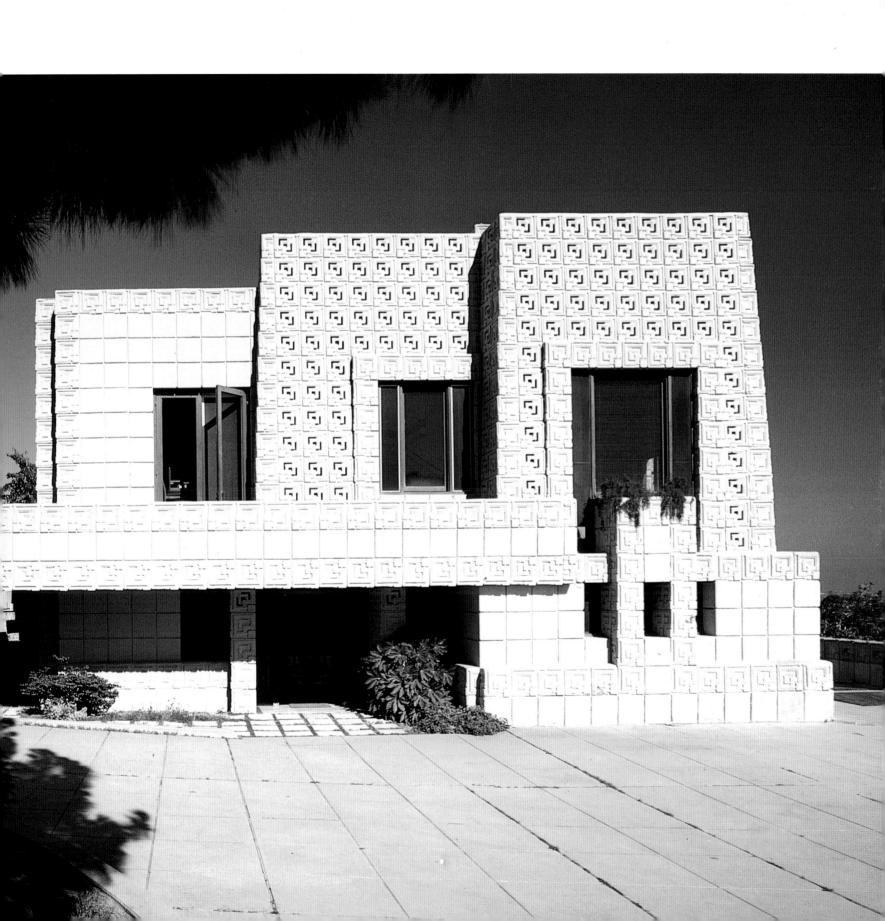

◀ From a small, dark entry on the first level—a space whose ceiling is under seven feet—marble stairs ascend to the upper level. Prolonging the suspense, Wright forces one to step onto the landing and turn right before the large living and dining area comes into view. Inside the door at the top of the stairs is a closet with built-in drawers.

and in many variations, depending on their intended use. These twenty-four variations create active surfaces that change unpredictably and pleasurably from exterior to interior and room to room. Textured blocks compose entire walls or are laid in rows that alternate with courses of solid block, or outline windows and doors, or are juxtaposed with perforated blocks. On whatever surface the eye falls, it is led up or down a column, along a wall, or around a corner.

Wright's art-glass windows and doors for the Ennis house, his most extensive use of art glass in any California building, contrast their delicate transparency with the solidity of the textile blocks. The imagery is believed to have been inspired by the trees originally on the site, such as short-needle pines and a wisteria that grew in the garden terrace on the north side of the house. A more realistic rendering of the wisteria appears in a mosaic over the fireplace designed by Wright and carried out by Orlando Giannini. The leaves and pale lavender blossoms hang gracefully from the gnarled branches and through a field of gilt tesserae.

Charles and Mabel Ennis requested that Wright change some of the materials he had chosen. Wright wanted to use slate for the floor of the colonnade, but the Ennises preferred marble. They also requested that the ceilings, floors, and door and window frames be finished in teak rather than redwood. Wright agreed to these substitutions, but the Ennises also wanted to alter the design of the living-room and dining-room ceiling, which called for a pitched soffit and teak strips that lined up with the joints of the textile blocks. The Ennises got what they wanted, and Wright refused to continue working on the house. The Ennises made their own decisions about other details. They commissioned Julian Dietzmann, a local craftsman, to make the iron gates at the street entrance to the courtyard. They also installed a Tiffany lamp in the dining room and hanging lamps of unknown origin along the colonnade.

Later owners also altered the house. Lloyd Wright, who supervised the initial construction, returned in the early 1940s to oversee two of his father's redesigns for a new owner, John Nesbitt: the addition of a swimming pool to the garden terrace and the conversion of a storage room on the ground floor into a billiard room.

Since 1968, August O. Brown, the seventh owner, has sought to conserve the house by embarking on such projects as restoring the garden between the Ennises' bedrooms, which had been turned into a bathroom and third bedroom. With the ongoing restoration efforts have come discoveries about the house: the bathroom ceilings were originally painted gold, and the mosaic tiles on the floor in front of the fireplace were also gold. One of the theories to emerge is that the Ennis block design is a rhythmic visual interpretation of the warp and woof of textiles, a reference to the clients' clothing business. The myths and legends that continue to surround the house remain as tantalizing as the architecture itself.

▲ Reaching the upper floor from the entry level below, one arrives at the beginning of the loggia, and at what initially seems to be a maze of textile-block columns and beams.

◀ The loggia, opening up to become part of the living room, frames the fireplace and the mosaic mural above it. To the right of the hearth is a long, tall closet, over thirteen feet high, designed for the storage of ladders.

▶ A tall art-glass window in the dining room treats guests to a view of the city. Two corner windows of mitered glass, on the south side of the dining room, are among Wright's first uses of glass to dissolve the corner of a room.

▲ The elevated dining room has a full view of the nearly twenty-two-foot-high living room, the fireplace set within the loggia, and the continuation of the loggia along the north side of the house. Wright referred to this part of the house as "The Great Room." The doors at right lead to the bedroom once used by Mabel Ennis.

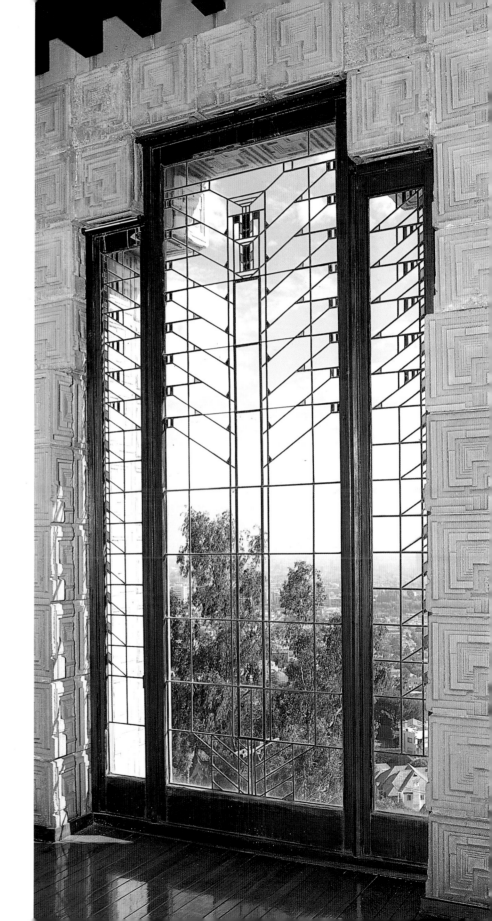

▲ Wright contrasts the solidity of concrete blocks with the subtly colored geometry of art glass. Here, an exterior wall of perforated textile blocks can be seen through one of the clerestory windows in the loggia.

▲ The doors from the living room to Mabel Ennis's bedroom reiterate the abstract design used in the windows on the opposite side of the room. As well as decorative, the treatment serves as a curtain between public and private spaces.

◄ Charles Ennis's bedroom is at the east end of the house, across the garden terrace from his wife's. Outside the door and its narrow flanking windows is a small terrace. The angled corners of the room reflect the battered walls on the exterior. This bedroom is the only one with a fireplace.

# STORER RESIDENCE

## 1923 • Hollywood

O f Wright's four textile-block houses in Los Angeles, the John Storer residence presents itself the most straightforwardly, the most accessibly, without the suspenseful transition the architect often contrived between exterior and interior. Situated above street level and set into a slope in the Hollywood hills, the residence is reached by ascending two banks of stairs to a front courtyard, to the accompaniment of a fountain splashing into a small pool. Along the first level of the facade, five redwood-framed glass doors alternate with textile-block columns that rise in between the second-story windows. The doors open not into a compressed space like a foyer or corridor but right into the spacious, light-filled dining room.

One immediately feels drawn through the house as if borne on the free flow of air and light. As at the Millard residence, the dining room and the second-level living room directly above it make up the central mass of the house. But whereas the Millard's living areas face southwest, the Storer's enjoy both northern and southern exposures, with numerous windows and glass doors that suffuse the two floors with sunlight and lighten the heaviness of the concrete blocks. The sense of graceful, fluid circulation invites movement not only from floor to floor and room to room but from the interior back out to the exterior. The over three-thousand-square-foot interior space is surrounded by almost as many square feet of courtyards and terraces. All of the rooms open to the outdoors: the front bedroom to the entry terrace, the rear bedroom to the swimming-pool courtyard, the dining room to both, the living room to pavilions on either side.

▲ Four of the different blocks used throughout the house—a perforated cruciform pattern, plus corner, coping, and plain blocks—appear at this corner of the retaining wall. Here, as at the other textile-block houses, the sixteen-inch-square blocks were cast from decomposed granite found on the site.

◄ Entering the house from the front courtyard brings one directly into the dining room. The original concrete-block floor was later surfaced with poured concrete, which was subsequently scored to continue the grid established by the blocks on the entry terrace. Standing lamps in bronze tubing, now painted black—two of which are shown here—and several hanging lamps are Wright's only furniture designs for the house. The dining-room table, also a Wright design, was made for the 1908 Isabel Roberts residence in Oak Park. To the left of the table is the door to the kitchen.

▼ Storer residence, viewed from the south. The central mass contains the dining room on the ground level, the living room on the second level. The bedrooms are to the left at split-levels.

Despite the appearance of the house from the facade, the interior actually has four levels, each of which offers its own spatial experience. Treated as intimate refuges from the public spaces, the four small bedrooms are mirror images located above one another at split-levels below the living room and above the dining room. The dining room accommodates a dining area at the east end, adjacent to the kitchen and attached servant's quarters, as well as a sitting area around the textile-block fireplace nearer the center of the room. The living room is the only room on the second main level and, with its flanking terraces, seems to float above the rest of the house. In the plans, Wright had intended to "levitate" the living room within its textile-block shell by extending the floor only to the columns and not all the way to the north and south walls. But in the execution, the floor was completed conventionally.

After Dr. John Storer, the original client, died, the house was changed, in some ways drastically, by subsequent owners. In the 1970s Lloyd Wright, who had supervised the initial construction and landscaping, returned at the request of the new owner to restore the interior woodwork and textile blocks, which had been painted over. He also designed a pool for the rear terrace and added forced-air heating to augment the electrical heating his father had provided. The pool was finally built in the 1980s by the current owner, who embarked on an extensive restoration effort, supervised by Eric Lloyd Wright, and who furnished the house with pieces Wright had designed for other residences.

One of the projects was to restore the two canvas awnings to the second-level terraces. Lloyd Wright had designed awnings for the original house with the approval of his father. Research of the elder Wright's drawings uncovered a colored rendering that showed awnings supported by copper columns, which were re-created in favor of the Lloyd Wright design. Wright's awnings colorfully describe the spaces but do not close them off from the tree-sheltered property and distant views. Although the Storer house does not occupy a large, lushly wooded site as the Millard does or a dramatic hilltop as the Ennis does, Wright's deft handling of the multiple levels, outside and in, and of the balance between glass and textile block simultaneously offers experiences of isolation and openness.

◄ ▲ Rows of perforated blocks (opposite) shield the front bedrooms from the stairs to the entry courtyard. They also bathe the interior with filtered light (above) and bring in air when the sliding, redwood-framed window is opened. When the identical window in the opposite bedroom, across the hall, is opened, north-south breezes refresh the west part of the house.

▶ All of the glass doors
on the ground floor
provide access to and
ventilation for the dining
room, but the fourth one
from the left is the
formal entry. From the
facade, it is possible to
see that the living room,
on the second level, has
a higher ceiling than the
dining room.

▶ The blue canvas awning over the west terrace is supported by
columns of redwood and articulated copper that extend to the eaves.
Copper diamonds hold the awning slides. The side panels are edged
in Cherokee red, as are the cream and blue panels of the awning on
the east terrace. The pattern of interlocking squares on this and the
other eaves was originally stenciled, rather than handpainted, and in
the plan continued on the living-room ceiling.

► Light streams into the living room from the east terrace doors as well as from the windows that fill the north and south walls. The oak floors are stained to match the redwood ceiling, beams, and window mullions. Lloyd Wright's table and barrel chairs for the 1926 Sowden residence in Los Angeles are to the left of the terrace doors.

◄ Wright-designed furniture is arranged around the living-room fireplace, which shares the textile-block core of the dining-room fireplace on the floor below. The sofa and matching armchair are re-creations of the furniture for the Imperial Hotel, and the tables, with Wright's characteristic motif of interlocking geometric shapes, date from 1955. The stairs between the two floors are located behind the fireplace, and the stairs in the distance lead up and out the double doors to the west terrace.

► To reach the bedrooms, one leaves the light-filled living spaces and enters this dark stairwell. Because the bedrooms are a split-level below the living room, openings in the textile-block wall allow one to look back into the living and dining rooms.

# FREEMAN RESIDENCE
## 1923 • Los Angeles

**W**right's smallest textile-block house, a residence for Samuel and Harriet Freeman, also makes the most understated first impression. From the street, or north side, it appears to be simply a one-story structure with a detached garage. The solid block wall along the courtyard and the placement of the entry at the east end of it tantalizingly hide some of the most notable features—the lower level and terrace set into the hillside and the massing of the concrete-block volumes, with two stories of corner windows that offer views of the wooded site and the city beyond it—leaving them to be discovered as one moves into and through the house.

In size, plan, and impact, the living room dominates the interior. Of the total fifteen hundred square feet, it occupies nearly half, or slightly over seven hundred square feet. The space clearly has two focuses of attention. One, the area around the hearth—framed by the two textile-block beams and piers that divide the room into three parts—is dark and cloistered. The other, a south-facing wall of glass opposite the fireplace, is open and expansive. Mitered glass windows, which continue uninterrupted to the ground-floor bedrooms, dissolve the southeast and southwest corners of the room and give the concrete-block massiveness an uplifting lightness. Wright's early use of visible mitered glass is accompanied by another innovation that would become a common feature in his residential designs two decades later: the Freeman kitchen is adjacent to the combined dining/living area rather than next to servants' quarters or a separate formal dining room.

Lloyd Wright supervised the construction of the Freeman house, serving

▲ Freeman residence, viewed from the north side. The main entrance is on the right under the loggia. The garage and attached apartment are to the left.

▶ While the south side of the living room looks outward, the north side is dark and contained. Rudolf Schindler designed the unusual low seating and attached shelves. The wood is gum.

as both project architect and contractor. He also specified the location of plantings added to the eucalyptus trees already on the site. After the Freemans occupied the house, Rudolph Schindler became their architect for over two decades. Schindler, who had worked with Wright on the Imperial Hotel in Tokyo and the Barnsdall house in Los Angeles, made various modifications to suit the Freemans' use of the residence for cultural gatherings and for long-term visits by their artistic friends such as Edward Weston.

On the first floor, Schindler removed Wright's wall between the kitchen and living room—which included a pass-through window and fold-down counter—and replaced it with a doorway and a wall of shelving. Among his other contributions to the living space were a pair of low sofas—one that folds out, another that is cantilevered—placed perpendicular to the fireplace wall. Schindler reconfigured the ground-floor bedrooms into apartments and added furniture of his own design. The space below the garage, originally a laundry connected to the house by a covered terrace, was converted to an apartment which the Freemans used as a rental unit.

In 1986, Harriet Freeman moved out of the house, which she had donated three years earlier to the University of Southern California. Since then the USC School of Architecture has been studying the building in considerable depth. Among the discoveries is that Wright created over fifty variations of the basic asymmetrical textile block he designed for the house. Some, like the use of mirror images, are more obvious than others, like the castings made for various miters. The pattern on the Freeman block is a particularly complex design compared with those in the other southern California textile-block residences. One interpretation of the abstraction is that it represents the square floor plan of the house on its site, enveloped by the surrounding eucalyptus, which still stand today.

◄ The setting sun passing through the concrete-block clerestories patterns the east wall of the living room. As predictably as a sundial, the morning sun comes through the opposite clerestories. At the left side of the built-in shelving is a door that leads to the kitchen. The octagonal table, designed by Wright, was originally taller and could be fitted into the wall outside the kitchen.

▼ The house is oriented on the site so that it frames a view south down Hollywood's Highland Avenue. Outside the double doors and dropped down three steps is a small balcony. The ceiling, in two levels, is Douglas fir.

◄ Floor-to-ceiling windows wrap around the south corners of the living area and continue, uninterrupted, to the living quarters on the floor below. The renowned architect John Lautner, who apprenticed with Wright, replaced the original wood mullions with aluminum. The ceiling fixture, a simple light box with a pane of glass inserted in the ceiling molding, is a Schindler design. The bronze standing lamp is one of three Wright created for the house.

▲ Lights are set behind the glass-filled perforated brick in the entry-court loggia.

◄ In the hallway that leads from the entry to the living room, in the distance, the only illumination comes from the light that filters from the courtyard area through the row of perforated bricks.

# HANNA RESIDENCE

## 1936 • Palo Alto

I n 1936, the same year Wright designed his first Usonian house—the Herbert Jacobs in Madison, Wisconsin—he planned for Paul R. and Jean S. Hanna his first residence in the northern part of California. The Hanna house exceeded the size of the Jacobs Usonian by over three thousand feet, therefore necessitating a much larger budget, but it still expresses the philosophical and aesthetic principles that Wright was beginning to define and would expand upon over the next two decades.

Challenged by what he described as the "American 'small house' problem," Wright sought to design "the modest dwelling for our time and place." The solution: a residence, generally one story, made affordable by the efficient use of space, materials, and construction techniques, without sacrificing aesthetics or sensitivity to the clients' needs. The main features: a spacious living room open to the surrounding landscape, a compact kitchen called a workspace, a dining area rather than a formal dining room, and a concrete-slab floor that carries a hot-water heating system.

An essential element of the Usonian design was a geometric module that determined the plan and construction. Inscribed on the concrete floor, it also appeared in a variety of structural and decorative details, in a range of scales, including light fixtures and furniture. For the unit system of the Hanna house—which was used to make concrete tiles rather than to inscribe a concrete floor—Wright turned to an efficient structure, the honeycomb, built by one of nature's architects. "I am convinced," he wrote, "that a cross-section of

▲ Hanna residence, viewed from the west. Rising above the roofline is the central masonry core containing the living-room fireplace. The roof, now composition, was originally copper. Differences in the roof planes reflect variations in interior ceiling heights, from slightly under seven feet to just over sixteen.

▶ The honeycomb plan, with its 120-degree angles, creates a fluid, organic relationship between interior and exterior and from one material to another.

honeycomb has more fertility and flexibility where human movement is concerned than the square."

Wright applied the hexagonal unit system so that the Honeycomb House, as it came to be called, spreads organically rather than intrusively across its site. In the decades since the house was built, the shade trees have reached upward and outward to further claim the residence as part of the landscape. The absence of right angles promotes movement from one room to another and from interior to exterior. Every main room of the house, except the kitchen, opens onto one of the garden terraces, which continue, without interruption, the hexagonal unit system of the floor.

Because Wright's furniture follows the same system, it makes efficient use of space. In the living room, built-in bench seating allows one to enjoy the warmth of a fire in the sunken hexagonal hearth or to appreciate the view of one of the front garden terraces. Hexagonal floor cushions and hassocks can be moved where needed or tucked out of sight. The bedrooms were outfitted with beds based on the hexagonal unit, which therefore require custom mattresses. For the bathrooms, Wright specified the use of sunken tubs, another way to increase the sense of space.

The Hannas, who obtained a long-term lease on the land from Stanford University, where Paul Hanna taught, wanted the ultimately adaptable house, one that would accommodate both family and professional functions and could be altered as their lives changed. Anticipating the Hannas' needs, Wright designed the interior so that screws could be removed from the horizontal battens, soffits, and other woodwork, and the rooms reconfigured. In the mid-1950s, following Wright's plan, the Hannas converted the study and master bedroom into a library, and created a new master bedroom by combining two of the smaller bedrooms. The other modifications they made during their years in the house include the addition, in 1953, of guest quarters and a workshop, which wrap around the northeast

▼ The sliding door of the playroom, which is dropped down one step from the main house, can be opened to eliminate the separation between indoors and outdoors. When their children grew up, the Hannas used the playroom as a dining room. Trellises extend over planting areas that act as a transition from the house to the terrace.

◀ Throughout the house, windows and doors angle outward onto the terraces in conformation with the hexagonal unit system.

▼ The bedrooms face an inner garden terrace away from the street, ensuring the occupants' privacy.

corner of the site to embrace the inner garden and terraces. A garden house and pool designed by John Howe, one of Wright's apprentices, were built in 1960 under the supervision of William Wesley Peters.

In the many letters the Hannas wrote to Wright during the design and construction process, they fretted about their ability to afford the unexpected cost overruns but remained committed to Wright's vision and the completion of the house. When the architect walked in the door just after the Hannas moved in, he said to them, "We have created a symphony here." The Hannas lived in Wright's masterpiece of spatial rhythm through 1974, when they bequeathed the house to Stanford University.

# BAZETT-FRANK RESIDENCE

## 1939 • Hillsborough

For the second house Wright designed in northern California, he again showed that the honeycomb could be used to create spaces that are visually provocative, unusually fluid in their interrelationship, and functionally suited to the Usonian concept. As well as sharing these attributes with its predecessor, the Hanna house, the Bazett uses similar materials, namely brick, redwood, and concrete. Otherwise, there are significant distinctions between the two in size and layout and in overall effect.

At less than half the floor area of the Hanna house, the Bazett is configured in two wings—one for the bedrooms, the other for the living space—which embrace a terrace before opening onto an expanse of lawn. At what could be called the vertex of the wings is a masonry core that encloses the compact kitchen but still permits a view through the kitchen doorway into the dining area and out a wall of windows into the garden. "My sense of the wall was no longer the side of a box," Wright later wrote about his quest to build the "new" house. "It was the enclosure of space. . . . But it was also to bring the outside world into the house and let the inside of the house go outside." As this idea is expressed at the Bazett house, the living/dining wing meets the garden and terraces along a series of ceiling-high glass doors and windows that angle inward and outward in satisfying conformation with the hexagonal plan. More screen than wall, they

▲ The carport roof soffit steps back at the entrance to the studio/guest wing. Recessed triangular lights are found on the interior as well as the exterior of the house.

◀ From the carport, there are two main entrances to the house. This one opens into a foyer; the other, to its left, opens directly into the living room. Horizontally raked brick is used throughout the residence.

▲ Bazett-Frank residence, viewed from the west. The bedroom wing is to the left, the living area to the right.

activate the space with their rhythm as well as diminish the boundary between interior and exterior.

The volumes and rhythms of the hexagon plan are stated with particular assertiveness in the bedroom wing, which actually consists of two cleverly compact suites with connecting bedrooms, dressing rooms, and baths. A single hexagon unit—really a cubicle—serves as a transitional "hallway" between the public foyer and the private suites. The rooms are small and cabinlike, but they do not seem cramped because of the 60-degree and 120-degree angled walls and the furniture built into them. The form of each feature is determined by the unit system: the stainless-steel bath and shower tubs and the skylights, for instance, are single hexagons; the beds and couches, double hexagons.

Whereas the Hannas changed the Honeycomb House throughout their tenure, the Bazett house remains largely as it was when the client, Sidney Bazett, and the builder, Blaine Drake, completed it. The Bazetts lived in the house only briefly, however, and Louis J. and Elizabeth Frank bought it in 1945 and have faithfully maintained the residence as if they were the original clients. In 1954, the Franks asked Wright to design an addition for the guest

▼ Once inside the foyer, one can descend to the left into the dining/living area, turn right at the wall with the sawn-wood windows into the bedroom wing, or step through the glass doors onto the garden terrace.

quarter, located across the carport from the main house. The room, another suite, has built-in beds, shelving, cabinets, and its own bath, all extending beautifully, organically, of course, from the original hexagonal system.

Wright, who was so often prescient throughout his life, oriented the house on the one-acre site so that some rooms have views of the San Francisco Bay to the east while others look out onto the lawn and garden. Although the Bazett-Frank house is no longer the only structure on its ridge in Hillsborough, south of San Francisco, it still offers the same two experiences: the ability to survey the world from a distance and the sense of being secluded within one's own world.

▲ The fireplace is set asymmetrically into the masonry core that contains the kitchen. To the right, up the stairs and under the soffit, is the entrance to the living area from the carport. To the left is the kitchen doorway and beyond that the foyer. Changes in ceiling height promote the pleasing flow from one space to another.

◄ A long wall of built-in seating looks across the dining/living room and out to the garden. The continuous band of sawn-wood windows not only patterns the wall with light but also makes the soffit seem weightless. Wright designed the multipart dining table to fit the wall of windows opposite the hearth or to be disassembled and the units used individually. Glass doors at the end of the room lead onto a low-walled terrace.

▲ The windows and doors of the living area project onto the terrace, emphasizing the closeness, rather than the separation, of inside and outside.

▶ The compact, cabinlike bedroom suites have built-in beds and couches. Each piece is the size of two hexagonal units and requires customized mattresses.

▲ Patterned, sawn-wood windows provide light and, when open, air into the bedroom suites.

◄ Bath and shower tubs were custom-made of stainless steel to fit the hexagonal plan.

# STURGES RESIDENCE

## 1939 • Los Angeles

**W**right's masterpiece Fallingwater naturally comes to mind when one looks up at the George D. Sturges residence, his first Usonian in southern California, suspended over its hillside lot in the Brentwood Heights section of Los Angeles. The entire floor area of the house could easily fit inside the Fallingwater living room with plenty of space left over, and its location is less spectacular than the Fallingwater rural landscape. These and other distinctions aside, Wright used the dramatic cantilever here not only to create a distinctive relationship between building and site but also to make ingenious and practical use of limited interior space combined with exterior terraces.

At the Sturges house, the cantilever floats the living room, bedrooms, and deck over the site, and gives occupants a significant measure of separation from the street and from their neighbors. The residence is reached from the street by a short driveway that rises to a carport and a covered entry courtyard. From this approach and from the driveway, the redwood siding and masonry core are the outstanding features of the house. Horizontality predominates—in the overlapped redwood boards and in the raked brick—and emphasizes the thrust of the cantilever.

The entrance, at the northwest corner of the house, just off the carport, opens into the living room. In a juxtaposition Wright commonly used in living areas, a masonry core with a fireplace faces a wall of glass. Outside this glass wall—actually three adjoining glass doors—is a generous deck that runs along the south side of the house and wraps around the east side to join the

▲ Sturges residence, viewed from the east.

▶ The fireplace is set slightly off center in the masonry wall of the living room. Continuing the horizontal lines of the raked brick, the shelving wraps around the dining alcove.

▶ Running along the south side of the house, the deck can be accessed from the living room, in the foreground, and the bedrooms, in the distance. The trellis, formed by extensions of the laminated redwood ceiling beams, creates a feeling of enclosure while remaining open to the sky. Cutouts in the redwood trellis supports give the trellis a lift.

▼ Wright designed the cushioned plywood chairs for use with the dining-room table.

forecourt. The bedrooms, also facing south, enjoy deck views and access. A deck on the roof and a workshop below the main floor, within the cantilever structure, expand the living space.

Wright provided both built-in and freestanding furniture for the original clients. Shelves extend from the fireplace and along the wall outside the kitchen to create an alcove for the dining area. John Lautner, who supervised construction of the house, designed the dining-room table, for use with Wright's dining-room chairs. Wright provided built-in beds for the two bedrooms, which were later removed by a subsequent owner.

The cantilevering of the house and deck, impressive on their own, are even more striking in their effect and satisfying in their proportions with Wright's inclusion of a trellis. The trellis, formed by the ceiling beams piercing through the south wall, runs along the front of the house. The overlapping boards and battered corners of the deck rail project even farther, adding to the residence's dynamic profile.

▼ Decorative articulated columns connect the laminated beams with the ceiling. All elements are redwood.

▶ Two armchairs designed by Wright for the original clients are made of vertical-grain, Douglas fir plywood that looks as if it has been folded from a single plywood sheet. The chairs are modeled after the architect's well-known versions for Taliesin West. The tonalities of the furniture, the redwood walls and ceiling, and the masonry warm the living room.

# OBOLER GATEHOUSE AND STUDIO-RETREAT

### 1940–41 • Malibu

A small dwelling perched like a lookout atop a hill high above the Pacific Ocean serves as a poignant guardian over Wright's partially realized vision for Arch Oboler. Oboler, a major figure in the golden age of radio, had already launched his career when he acquired several hundred acres along a remote, scenic ridge in Malibu. He commissioned Wright to design for him and his family an estate with a gatehouse, a studio, a main house, and other features. Construction of the complex was delayed by various factors, including the redesign of the main house. A succession of Wright's apprentices—one of them John Lautner—supervised the project, and Aaron Green of Wright's San Francisco office occasionally came to Los Angeles to advise Oboler. What ultimately halted further progress was the death of one of the Obolers' young children in a tragic accident on the site where the masonry walls for the main house had just begun to be built. Only three of the structures were ever completed.

With the use of rubblework at Taliesin West still fresh in his mind, Wright must have sensed that rough-hewn stone and mortar would be as suitable for the California coastal mountains as it was for the Arizona desert. Wright's approach would have been to select rocks indigenous to the region. Oboler, however, an enthusiastic rockhound, gathered the rocks from a variety of locations, even driving his van to the Arizona desert around Taliesin West to collect rocks like those Wright had used for his own residence. As a result of Oboler's eclectic tastes, pieces of brilliant stone, in aquamarine or yellow,

▲ The Oboler studio-retreat faces east to accept the morning light. The main approach to the building is up the ridge, by the trees, and along the masonry wall, which momentarily hides the view to the ocean. Cantilevered slightly from its anchoring masonry core, the studio-retreat is visually grounded by the horizontal lines of the overlapped boards and roof overhang.

▲ Sited so that it does not
obstruct the view of the
mountains from the entrance
drive, the gatehouse is
connected by a porte cochere
to another low building,
which includes bedrooms
and workspaces.

◄ To reach the main entrance
to the gatehouse, one
proceeds through the porte
cochere and walks along the
building toward the terrace.
This approach offers a view
of the pool and the hills
receding to the west.

77

▼ The fireplace is part of the masonry core that anchors the studio-retreat to its site. To the right is the main doorway, which when closed fits like a puzzle piece into the battered door frame. The sawn-wood openings over the ceiling lights have the same pattern as the louvered windows of the gatehouse.

shine out from walls, walkways, and terraces that also contain a rich palette of tans, grays, and earthy reds. Nevertheless, seen altogether laid up in masonry walls, Oboler's multicolored collection effectively grounds the buildings physically and unites them esthetically with the rugged, scrubby landscape.

The first residence Wright designed for the Obolers, bearing the poetic name Eagle Feather, was intended to be built on a ridge, from which it would cantilever dramatically toward the ocean, thrusting a seemingly weightless terrace into space. Objecting to the lavishness of the design, the Obolers asked Wright to create a simpler residence located near the gatehouse. Since the main house was never completed, the Obolers lived in the gatehouse, a modest-sized residence with a living room, a kitchen, and a bedroom. Complementing the masonry core and walls, redwood is used on the exterior walls and fascia, on the interior ceilings and battered walls, and for the built-in benches and shelves in the living room. The interior seems dark and confined, but the climate and beauty of the surroundings—and the convenience of an adjacent terrace and pool—make the outdoors inviting the year around. Across the driveway from the gatehouse and connected to it by a porte cochere is a long, rectangular building with the children's bedrooms, all of them well supplied with built-in furniture. Whereas both these buildings sit low on the site in order to preserve the contours of the landscape and the panoramic views, the small, one-room studio-retreat for Oboler's wife, Eleanor, is an aerie at one of the high points on the property. Rather than face west, it looks east, its wall of windows surveying the seemingly endless layers of mountain silhouettes.

Arch and Eleanor Oboler lived in the gatehouse and other buildings for many years. By the end of his career, Oboler had authored over eight hundred dramas for radio, a medium he described as the "theater of the mind." He also was acknowledged as the first writer to have his radio plays appear on his own national network series and was recognized as the writer and director of the first significant three-dimensional movie. After he died in 1987, Eleanor remained briefly on the property, then sold it to a new owner, who plans eventually to restore Wright's buildings.

◄ Unlike the other buildings, which look west, the studio-retreat faces east toward the mountains and canyons high above the Malibu coast.

◄ The only natural light in the studio-retreat bathroom comes from a skylight whose shape reiterates that of the small space.

# WALKER RESIDENCE

## 1948 • Carmel

▲ Walker residence, viewed from
the southwest.

▶ A ship's prow is a fitting image for the
terrace, which launches over the rocky
shoreline and looks out across the bay.
Whereas the copper roof extends to meet
the terrace wall, the windows step inward
toward the masonry wall of the living room.
The stairs at left descend to the beach.

Throughout his career, Wright was asked to design several houses for locations on the coast of California, but the Walker residence is the only commission that was ever realized. Della Walker did not want an extravagant residence, but her site on the rocky shoreline of Monterey Bay offered Wright an extravagance of nature's riches. After seeing her piece of coastline with its commanding view of the Pacific Ocean, he began work on what he called in his letters a "cabin on the rocks."

The finished house, clearly more elegant in appearance than Wright's nickname might imply, is a Usonian plan whose features take maximum advantage of the spectacular location without overwhelming it. A terrace, in the appropriate shape of a ship's prow, projects over the shoreline, appearing at once to emerge from the rocks and sand and to reach out to the sea. From inside the house, there are many views celebrating the panorama, so that the ocean never seems very far away.

In orientation, size, and configuration, the living room is the center of the twelve-hundred-square-foot residence. Abutting the terrace, it is a large hexagon, five sides of which have continuous bands of metal-framed windows. Because of the 120-degree angles of the adjoining walls, the three walls of built-in bench seating look both outdoors and toward the fireplace in the masonry core, which also forms one side of the kitchen. The dining area, located just outside the kitchen, was designed to include a built-in table, which Walker requested that Wright make freestanding. The two guest bedrooms and master bedroom occupy a wing between the living area and the

▲ A concrete walkway, continuing the sixty-degree triangular unit system Wright used throughout the house, leads from the carport to the main entry. The baffles give the interior some privacy but do not block the view. Cedar, the choice of the original client, was used on the exterior and for the interior walls and furniture.

◀ Mitered glass permits an uninterrupted view through the corner living-room windows, which open downward rather than outward. The color of the mullions, Wright's favorite red, contrasts exquisitely with the copper roof.

carport. The master bedroom, at the east end of the house, was enlarged in 1960 by San Francisco architect Sandy Walker, Della Walker's grandson.

Wright's other design decisions responded to the topography and climate. The windows in the living room and the bedrooms, stepping out from the masonry walls in horizontal panes, open downward rather than outward to protect the interior from gusty onshore winds. Deep roof overhangs shade the windows as well as the walkway along the south side of the house from the carport to the main entrance. Whereas the copper roof blends into the sky, the pale tonalities of the stonework merge with the sand and indigenous rock.

The copper roof, visible from the shore as well as from out in the water, has long been a hallmark of the residence, but was added several years after Wright's death to replace the original roof, which was enameled steel. Construction of the Walker house did not begin until a few years after Wright designed it. Walter Olds, who had supervised the building of the Buehler house, and Aaron Green of Wright's San Francisco office were involved with various stages of the construction. By the time work on the Walker residence had begun, copper was scarce because of the Korean War. After various alternatives were considered, a way was found to use enameled steel. Because color choice was important in order to imitate copper patina, various shades were tested. Upon reviewing the samples, Wright made a brilliant decision: to use a combination involving all the colors so that the roof would not seem uniformly flat, but would be as richly varied as the stone and wood he had selected.

▼ Wright's dynamic design for the gate was executed in cedar, as was the interior and exterior of the house. The stone, a local variety called Carmel stone, was obtained from a quarry in the area.

# BUEHLER RESIDENCE

### 1948 • Orinda

▲ The main entrance is at the end of the walkway along a row of sawn-wood windows placed high enough that they block a view of the interior. The roof overhang shelters the walkway, and its soffit contains lights that illuminate the passageway at night. To the right in the distance is the cantilevered roof of the living room.

**M**ystery and anticipation, whether expressed on the grand scale of the Ennis house or on the more modest scale of a Usonian, were qualities important to Wright when he conceived the kind of experience his buildings would promote. The residence of Maynard P. and Katherine Buehler, a Usonian, discloses little about itself from its public approach and only reveals itself gradually, in stages, progressing from dark to light, from contraction to expansion.

The short driveway, at the end of a cul-de-sac in the San Francisco Bay Area community of Orinda, gently rises to two carports. Beginning underneath one of the carports, a long, narrow walkway runs along the north side of the house and under the roof overhang. The space just inside the entrance is equally compact, with a low ceiling that is just six feet, eight inches high. This point of compression dramatically expands into a large octagonal living room. Its ceiling slopes upward from the entrance to reach an apex of fourteen feet where it meets a wall of windows. Visible through the windows, and through the nearby dining room, are the gardens and lush woods that seclude the residence from its neighbors.

Wright had the contours of the site graded so that the two wings of the four-thousand-square-foot house would sit on a gentle rise and face west and south onto the three-and-one-half acres, which are traversed by a small stream. The main wing contains three bedrooms and a den in addition to the dining and living rooms and kitchen. The smaller wing is a machine shop, which Wright designed especially for Maynard Buehler, complete with fireplace and built-in

◀ Only part of the entry walkway along the north side of the house is visible from the carport. The strong horizontality of the redwood board and batten encourages one to continue around the corner and proceed toward the main entrance.

▲ Buehler residence, viewed from the northwest. The living room is on the left, the workshop on the right.

▼ Alternating windows can be
opened to ventilate the interior
corridor that links the living area
and bedrooms.

cabinets. Both wings open onto terraces that surround a swimming pool, which was later made into the centerpiece of a Japanese garden.

Throughout the interior of the residence in particular, the coolness of the concrete block walls is warmed by the generous use of redwood and by the integrally colored, Cherokee red, polished concrete floor. From the board-and-batten walls to the perforations in the clerestory windows, all the woodwork is beautifully executed and supports the harmonious relationship of one room to another, of one ceiling height to another, of the windows to their frames. Wright designed a number of furniture pieces and built-ins for the house. Among them is the dining-room table and chairs in Honduras mahogany. The six separate triangular components of the table can be used singly or in a variety of different configurations. The backs of the chairs intentionally rise no higher than the tabletop so that they do not impede the view of the garden from the living-room seating. Manuel Sandoval, who made the cabinetry and furniture for the V. C. Morris Gift Shop, also crafted the Buehler pieces.

The Buehlers initially became acquainted with Wright's work through articles on his houses in *Architectural Forum.* After Wright consented to design a house for them, they met with him on one of the visits he made to the Bay Area to design the V. C. Morris Gift Shop. Wright saw the Buehlers' site, completed the plans, and recommended that Walter Olds, who was moving to California from Taliesin, supervise construction. The machine shop was built first, followed in 1949 by completion of the main house. In 1957, Olds designed a guesthouse that is compatible with the original residence and is set southwest of it, along the melodious stream.

◀ In contrast to the low entry, the
west side of the living room lifts
toward the sky. Underneath the
living room is a bedroom, which
makes this the only two-story part
of the house.

▶ Redwood planter boxes are set
along four of the living-room walls.
The supports at the junction of the
walls widen gradually from the floor to
the ceiling, the center of which is
covered in gold leaf.

▶ Mitered glass makes the corner of the dining room disappear and opens up the view of the hillside gently sloping toward the stream. To the right is a fireplace that shares its concrete-block core with the living-room fireplace. The coffered ceiling, originally glass, was later finished in gold leaf to match the living-room ceiling.

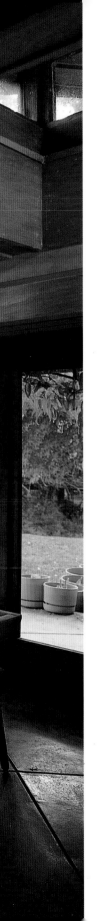

▲ One view from the dining room looks onto the Japanese garden and to the workshop beyond it. The table is set with reproductions of Wright's 1922 design for the dinnerware used in the cabaret room of the Imperial Hotel in Tokyo, Japan.

▶ The kitchen shelving and cabinetry terminate in a small built-in table of Honduras mahogany. To the left is the main entrance; to the right, the dining room, where a pass-through window gives convenient access to the kitchen.

# MORRIS GIFT SHOP

## 1948 • San Francisco

S mall in size but monumental in impact, the V. C. Morris Gift Shop clearly proves that customers can be enticed into a store without a flashy window display of merchandise as an advertisement. The Morrises did not build the store from the ground up but asked Wright to renovate a warehouse on a narrow lane in downtown San Francisco. His treatment of the facade in horizontally raked brick rather than glass makes the building stand out from its more conventional neighbors. Entrance to the store is through an archway placed provocatively off center. Leading passersby inside, a horizontal band of lights set below a line of pale bricks runs along the facade, turns sharply into the entrance along a low wall, and disappears into the store.

The sense of restraint on the exterior is promptly broken on the interior, a large, open space dominated by circles, arches, and curves. A ramp spirals gracefully from the ground floor to the upper level and allows numerous vantage points on the displays, anticipating Wright's design of the Guggenheim Museum in New York. The ceiling is covered by a matrix of concave and convex plastic lights, and the curved walls are punctured by portholes and decorative circular cutouts.

The Morrises wanted an elegant way to present their merchandise, which included china, glass, silver, linen, and other domestic items. To accommodate the need for both display and storage, Wright designed a number of freestanding and built-in pieces of furniture, executed in walnut by Manuel Sandoval, a Nicaraguan craftsman who had apprenticed with Wright. The walls on the upper level were lined with shelves, as was a back wall on the

▲ V. C. Morris Gift Shop, view of facade.

▶ Juxtaposing transparency and solidity, Wright made half of the entry brick and the other half glass to preserve the sheltering quality of the entrance while giving customers a full view of the store interior before they walk into the large, open space.

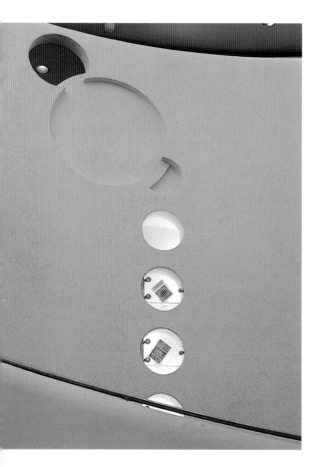

▲ The circular openings set in a
vertical row into the ramp wall
are small glass-faced display
cases with glass shelves that can
accommodate small decorative
objects and artworks.

ground floor. Although these were removed by later occupants of the building, much of the other original furniture remained intact. The low, semicircular tables and accompanying cushioned stools allowed the Morrises' clients to select, arrange, and contemplate various combinations of tableware. Lining one side of the store is a long, low set of drawers where objects not on display could be safely protected and easily accessed.

Wright gave the shop some unusual and delightful touches. A small gallery just inside the entrance to the left permits customers to sit quietly, away from the activity in the center of the store. To help shop personnel move merchandise from one floor to another, Wright provided a dumbwaiter. Some of the portholes in the walls are small display windows with shelves. Customers can stop as they walk up or down the ramp for a close-up view of a precious object in one of these intimate showcases. A concrete planter, suspended from the ceiling, echoes the large concave ceiling lights and is visible from both levels of the store.

The Morrises proved to be adventuresome clients. They commissioned Wright to design not only their gift shop but also three different residences— the most spectacular being a dramatic house sited in San Francisco on a cliff overlooking the Pacific Ocean. In the middle of the remodeling of their store, the Morrises were asked when they intended to start work on a house. They purportedly responded, "We can build only one masterpiece at a time." None of the residences was ever built, but the gift shop is surely one of Wright's significant legacies.

◀ Semicircular cutouts accent many of the pieces of furniture. Here, the cutout in the table base creates a seemingly delicate point over which the glass tabletop extends.

▼ The lights on the inside front wall of the store, above a walnut cabinet, are the same lights visible on the exterior. Bearing Wright's characteristic geometric detailing, the plastic coverings are not cast but are fabricated from separate pieces.

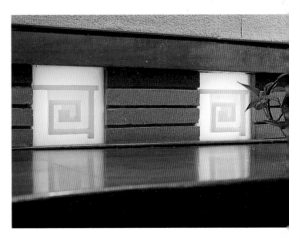

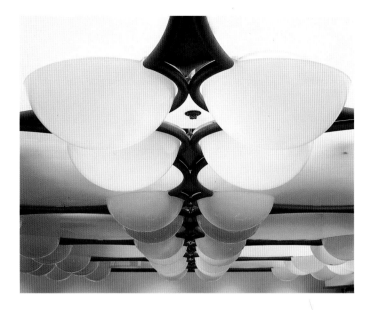

◀ Twenty-four large concave plastic disks, over six feet in diameter, seem anchored to the ceiling by a grid of ninety-six convex plastic bubbles.

▶ The shop's original owners used the low tables to display their fine tableware. Customers could sit and take their time considering arrangements of table settings. Manuel Sandoval, who crafted the furniture, also made the furniture and mural for Edgar J. Kaufmann's office at his department store in Pittsburgh, Pennsylvania.

◀ Wright inserted two levels of shelves under one of the circular tables.

# BERGER RESIDENCE

## 1950 • San Anselmo

Seen from the narrow road that winds up the hill, the rock-and-concrete walls of the Robert Berger residence rise sharply, even formidably, from the summit. From the front, however, the residence is more modest, yet equally intriguing. Although the one-story house is approximately sixteen hundred square feet, the front and side terraces, the various roof planes, and the deep overhangs make it look much larger and more spread out than it is across its hilltop site in San Anselmo, north of San Francisco.

When Robert Berger approached Frank Lloyd Wright to design a house for his family, he requested that it be one he himself could build. Berger's extensive engineering background impressed Wright, who dubbed him an "unfinished architect" and consented to take on the commission. Wright's confidence in his young client was justified, for Berger proceeded to construct the house largely by himself, from the masonry walls with their extra reinforcing to the built-in furniture. Aaron Green of Wright's San Francisco office advised Berger when necessary, especially with the detail work. In 1957, four years after construction began, Berger, his wife, Gloria, and their children moved into the still-unfinished house, sleeping in the living area until the bedrooms were finished. Completion of the house was in sight several years later when Berger became ill and passed away. His legacy of attentive and meticulous craftsmanship has contributed to making this residence a gem of Usonian design.

Of the two main sections of the house, one is centered around the hexagonal masonry core that literally and visually anchors the house to the

▲ Just beyond the triangular stonework pylon in the foreground and two steps down from the front terrace is the entrance to the house. The shape of the pylon and the scoring on the concrete terrace introduce the triangular module used throughout the plan. A band of sawn-wood windows set back from the wall plane lightens the visual weight of the roof and gives it the appearance of floating over the walls. The masonry core around which the living areas are organized rises prominently above the roof.

◄ The fireplace is the
nexus of the living area.
Its hob and grill reiterate
the angles of the hearth.
Radiating out from the
masonry core, the
ceiling seems to float
above the soffit.

▼ Berger residence,
viewed from the
southwest.

hill. Fanning out from this core, which contains a fireplace and a compact kitchen/workspace, is a broad living and dining area and a bedroom/study. A wing with two bedrooms extends east from the front entrance, its exterior masonry walls terminating dramatically in the point of a triangle. The house is oriented on its site so that the living areas and all the bedrooms have views of the foliage and distant hills.

The sixty-degree triangular module on which the plan is based recurs on many scales: in the lights set into the living-room soffit, in the diamond matrix scored on the concrete floor, in the overall shape of the terrace outside the living area. Further unifying the exterior and interior is the choice of materials. All the wood is Philippine mahogany. For the kitchen woodwork and for some built-in furniture, Berger chose a mahogany with a prominent ribbon stripe and carefully matched and aligned the pattern on each piece of furniture. By maximizing the use of space, the built-in seating, cabinetry, shelving, and tables of various sizes allow the interior to remain open and uncluttered. The stone selected for the masonry, a local variety called Santa Rosa stone, has pleasing muted pink tonalities that are compatible with the warm glow of the woodwork and the earthy red of the integrally colored, polished concrete floor—and with the surrounding terrain.

▲ A triangular light recessed into the roof soffit repeats the module Wright applied throughout the house.

▶ Two walls of windows, facing north and west, open the living area to the surrounding hills and valleys. They meet at a mitered-glass window whose angle is restated in the soffit. The built-in bench seating, originally intended for only one wall, was continued under all the windows. To the far right, in the distance, is the bedroom wing.

◀ Three six-sided tables, designed for the living area, fit together as one, or can be used individually. The three hexagonal stools can be tucked underneath them.

▼ Wright laid out the sawn-wood windows so that the end unit, with its mitered glass, wraps around the corner. The crisp geometry of the wood detailing contrasts with the textured irregularity of the concrete and stone.

▲ Shelves and built-in cabinets—all of which have piano hinges—line the walls beneath the band of windows. The patterned windows bring in natural light but guarantee privacy. This corridor leads from the bedroom wing to the front entrance, just to the left of the masonry wall in the background.

◄ The compact kitchen/ workspace is on the other side of the masonry core from the fireplace. A wall of shelving with a built-in table defines the dining area. Beyond the wall is a bedroom with shelving and built-in end tables. The doors at right lead to a terrace that projects outward, in Wrightian fashion, like the prow of a ship.

# MATHEWS RESIDENCE

## 1950 • Atherton

The period from the late 1940s until 1959, the last year of his life, was a prolific decade for Wright. A number of ambitious commissions occupied his time: the Guggenheim Museum in New York, the Price Tower in Oklahoma, the Butterfly Wing Bridge in California, and an opera house in Iraq. Many clients, including those in California, continued to seek out Wright for residences. To help him manage the volume of work, Wright asked Aaron Green, a former apprentice, to open an office in San Francisco. From 1951 through 1959, Green made the initial contact with clients, as when Randall and Harriet Fawcett walked into the Grant Avenue office one day to inquire about having Wright build their house in the Central Valley. Green also supervised the construction of Wright's buildings in California, such as the Pearce residence, and designed the landscaping for others, such as the Walton and Ablin residences. When Green opened the office in June of 1951, he started working on projects like the Walker residence, which Wright had already designed and were ready to build. Another was the house for Arthur C. Mathews and his wife, who had initially visited Wright at Taliesin to plan a residence for a site in Atherton, south of San Francisco.

Wright's design for the recently married couple suggests a synthesis of Prairie and Usonian concepts. The raked brick on the exterior of the angular U-shaped residence continues on the interior, where it is complemented with additional walls of redwood board and batten. Marked with the triangular unit system on which the house is based, the Cherokee red concrete floor extends from the exterior walkways and terraces into the interior. Wright outfitted the

▲ The glass walls of the living room, to the left, and the loggia, in the center, open onto a terrace on the east side of the house.

▼ Mathews residence, viewed from the southeast. The living area is to the left, the bedroom wing to the right.

▲ Openings in the roof overhang frame views of the sky and trees and bring light onto the terraces, which connect the interior spaces with the secluded landscape.

bedrooms and living areas with a full selection of built-in, Philippine mahogany furniture.

Like many of Wright's residences, the Mathews discloses little about itself from the main approach along the driveway to the carport. The character of the house changes, however, as one stands in front of the main entry, a glass door placed in between glass windows that reveal an enticing view straight through the interior to the wall of glass on the opposite side and the courtyard beyond. The two wings of the house—one for the bedrooms, the other for the living areas—embrace the courtyard. The entire residence is in turn surrounded and sheltered by the lush foliage and large, widely branching oak trees on the heavily wooded site.

# PEARCE RESIDENCE

### 1950 • Bradbury

As Wright designed an increasing number of Usonian houses throughout the 1940s, he explored various combinations of unit systems and
plans. One involved the use of arcs, singly and intersecting, as walls,
banks of windows, promenades, and terraces. Always seeking to work
with, rather than control, the elements of nature, Wright intended in this plan
to maximize the benefits of a dwelling's southern exposure. He described the
design as the solar hemicycle.

At the Wilbur C. Pearce residence in Bradbury, a suburb of Los Angeles,
the rooms are contained within the hemicycle or are configured around it.
As with all of Wright's hemicycle designs, the dominant feature is a long arc
of windows and glass doors along the south facade. At the Pearce house,
this nearly sixty-foot-long wall sweeps along the living room and the corri-
dor/gallery that leads to the master bedroom at the west end of the house. In
winter this wall of glass gathers the warmth of the sun. In summer the five
sets of double doors can be opened to provide cross-ventilation. And throughout the year, the house embraces copious natural light and a view of the
foothill country of the San Gabriel Mountains.

On the south side of the house, Wright fully exploits a play of concentric
and intersecting arcs to delineate the roofline and to describe a terrace, or
promenade as it is called on the plans, that curves outward from the living
area. An elliptical planting area, outlined by an arc of concrete blocks on the
promenade, acts as a transition from the living space to the surrounding hillside with its distinctive landscaping.

▲ Pearce residence, viewed from the
northeast. Set under the cantilevered carport
roof is a small terrace and the main entry.
To the left is a workshop; to the right is the
concrete-block core and the terrace outside
the dining area.

▶ Light streams into the living room from the south-facing wall of windows and glass doors off the terrace and from the glass doors of the dining area on the opposite wall. The three-foot-square unit of the design is scored on the polished concrete floor. The lights underneath the soffit just inside the terrace doors are also square.

◀ At its west end, the promenade off the living area terminates in double doors outside the master bedroom. The roof cantilevers over this part of the terrace, making it a small, shaded deck.

▲ Whereas the north side of the house emphasizes verticals and horizontals, the south side stresses the sweeping curves of the roofline and promenade.

▶ The two ceiling heights create a visual separation between the dining area and the living area and allow for clerestories. To the right of the fireplace is the main entry. The wall of floor-to-ceiling glass doors at the left opens onto a low-walled terrace. Tongue-and-groove Douglas fir was used for the ceiling; Honduras and Philippine mahogany for the woodwork and freestanding and built-in furniture.

Wright deftly carries out the hemicycle plan in the interior as well. The twenty-four-foot-long corridor from the living area to the bedroom enjoys a vantage onto the promenade and plantings. Along the curved interior wall of the corridor, Wright has placed a row of removable seats. The master bedroom, isolated at the west end of the house, has its own fireplace and dressing room. The built-in cabinets along the arced wall of the dressing room and the adjacent second bedroom circumvent the need for conventional angular furniture that would disrupt the fluid lines of the plan.

As in Wright's other Usonian houses, the kitchen and dining area are compact extensions of the living room. From the dining table and from the living room, it is possible to see the fireplace, set into an east wall just inside the main entrance. The living space opens to the north as well as to the south through three sets of floor-to-ceiling glass doors which front a terrace shaped by two low, arcing walls of concrete blocks. As he did so often and so well, Wright expanded the interior of the Pearce house by reaching out to the sky and the landscape.

▲ The approximately thirty-foot-long elliptical planting area outside the living space is formed by the concave wall of the house and the convex wall of the promenade. The sweeping arc of the roof is emphasized by the setback fascia boards, which are Douglas fir and pine.

# ANDERTON COURT SHOPS

## 1952 • Beverly Hills

Over four decades after they were built, the Anderton Court Shops in Beverly Hills still seem like part walk-through sculpture, part retail complex. Rather than using a conventional storefront facade pressed up to the street, Wright pulled the front of the concrete-and-glass building into the site to create a small entry court. This island offers passersby an oasis where they can pause away from the flow of pedestrian traffic to contemplate the displays in the shop windows or to observe the parade of people and vehicles on fashionable Rodeo Drive.

Whether or not the merchandise in the Anderton stores is enticing to prospective customers, Wright's asymmetrical design surely is. The six shops are stacked, three on each side of the building, and rather than occupying the same level, they are set a half floor above one another. Where the offset banks of shops meet at the front of the structure, two substantial piers support a ramp that accesses the various levels. The decorative tower that springs from the piers—an element Wright later repeated in the Marin County Civic Center—gives the building a distinctive identity from many vantage points.

When Nina Anderton approached Wright to design the shops, she intended at least one of them to showcase the work of a favored local couturier named Eric Bass. At Anderton's request, Wright included on the uppermost floor a two-bedroom residence where Bass would live. Shortly after the building's completion, Anderton and Bass had a falling-out, and the apartment was converted into another store. The living area of this "Usonian apartment" was designed to overlook Rodeo Drive and to open out onto a narrow landing with

▲ Large porthole windows in the shops on the north side look onto the passage that runs the length of the building on each floor. A small penthouse studio is set above the apartment at the back of the building.

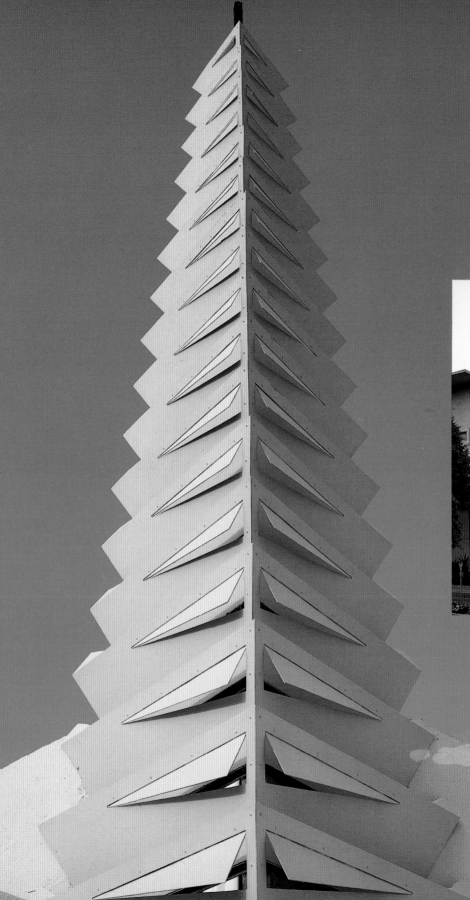

◄ The tower, like the soffit and fascia, is made of cast fiberglass that was tinted blue-green but later painted over. It was originally fitted with interior lights that projected their illumination through the louvers.

▲ Anderton Court Shops, viewed from Rodeo Drive.

109

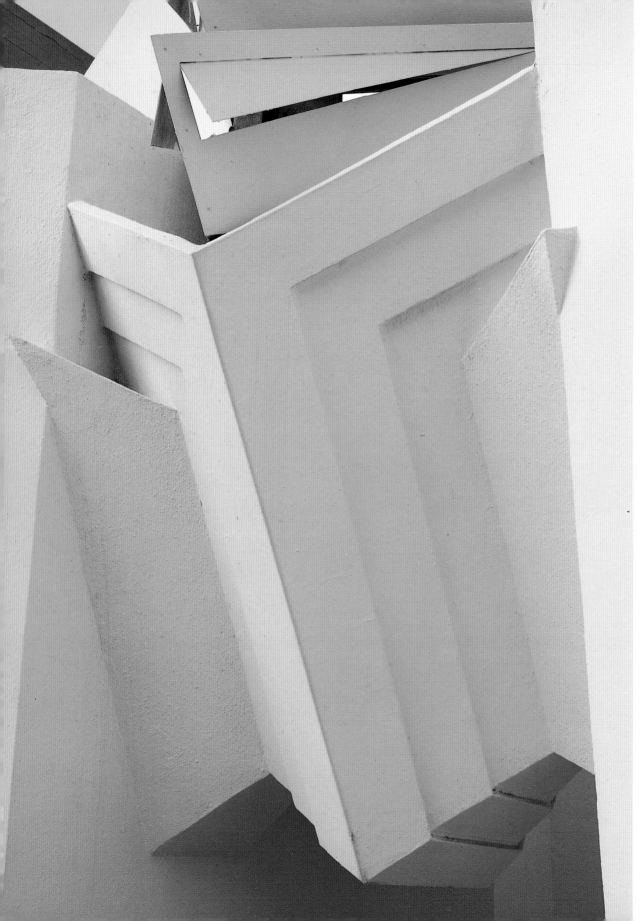

◀ The tower appears to telescope from the two central piers that support it and the ramp leading to the shops on the upper levels. The ornamental connection where the piers meet was not cast in concrete but was shaped by hand from gunite sprayed on the underlying form.

planting areas. As in Wright's Usonian houses of the time, the living and dining rooms of the apartment were merged into one large living space where the fireplace was a focal point and the kitchen was a small, efficient "workspace" adjacent to the dining area. Wright gave each of the five shops its own fireplace, a domestic feature he frequently incorporated in nonresidential buildings.

As a contrasting frame for the expanses of concrete and glass, Wright specified the use of decorative column covers, soffit panels, and fascia. These and the tower were to be made of copper, which would provide a striking contrast to the pale sandy color of the walls. After construction of the shops was under way, however, it became clear to Wright, Aaron Green of the San Francisco office, and Joe Fabris, Wright's on-site apprentice and the project contractor, that copper was prohibitively expensive. As an alternative, they chose molded fiberglass, a technology that had just begun to be used in boat building, and had the local fabricator impregnate the fiberglass with blue-green coloring to achieve the effect of copper patina. The construction of the roof also involved an approach innovative for Wright. Having recently redesigned the roof of Hillside Home School at Taliesin after a fire, he decided to apply the same technology to the Anderton Court Shops to increase the building's fire resistance. Concrete was poured over mesh-covered wood beams spaced four feet apart, and plaster was used for the interior finish.

As the basic unit for his plan, Wright chose a diamond, and the many scales and dimensions in which he expressed it—in the pattern incised on the poured concrete floor, in the structure of the central ramp and its parapets, in the ornamental detailing—contribute to the sculptural dynamism of the building. This quality advertises the building to people passing by on foot or in a car, and rewards all who further explore the court and its shops.

▼ The fascia and soffit, reminiscent of art deco motifs, was originally tinted blue-green to imitate the patina of copper. The cast fiberglass used here and for the column covers was later painted black or white. The walls, once a pale sandy color, are now white.

# KUNDERT MEDICAL CLINIC

## 1 9 5 5 • S a n   L u i s   O b i s p o

Karl Kundert became acquainted with Wright's work during the years he was a medical student at the University of Wisconsin at Madison. His firsthand experience of the architect's buildings in the Midwest, including a visit to Taliesin, remained strong memories after he moved to California. When he decided to construct a new clinic for his ophthamology practice in San Luis Obispo, a coastal city located between Los Angeles and San Francisco, Kundert asked Wright to take on the project.

Fulfilling Kundert's need for the features customarily found in medical buildings, Wright arrived at a solution that is at once straightforwardly practical and refreshingly inventive. The long, low, one-story building—in many senses a Usonian concept—shares a number of features with Wright's houses of the time: a plan based on the unit system, a harmonious and consistent use of materials, and a merging of indoors and outdoors through the inclusion of glass doors and windows and a garden terrace. At twenty-five hundred square feet, the clinic is not much larger than many of the architect's Usonian houses, but its massing and fenestration, and particularly the facade and entryway, subtly convey that this is an office, not a residence.

In the process of working on the clinic, Wright made a significant last-minute change. The completed plans called for the use of concrete block, not brick, along with Philippine mahogany for the woodwork and furniture. The foundations were about to be poured when Wright and the client met in his San Francisco office with Aaron Green, who was to oversee the construction. After reviewing the plans, Wright declared that the building would be much

▲ A mahogany slab that carries the building's address leads visitors to the main entry. The brick support and adjacent walls serve as a planter.

◄ Even when there isn't a fire burning in the fireplace, the hearth warms the interior of the clinic's waiting room. The doors at right lead to the terrace at the back of the building.

▲ Karl Kundert Medical Clinic, viewed from the west. To the right in the distance is the perpendicular wall that marks the main entrance.

▲ The overlapped mahogany boards and sawn-wood clerestories make the waiting-room ceiling soar. To the left of the reception desk is the main entrance to the building.

◄ The terrace, in Wright's ship's-prow shape, extends the reception area outdoors. Rising above the roofline is the masonry core that contains the fireplace, surrounded by the sawn-wood clerestory windows of the reception area.

more effective in raked brick, which, he confided, had been his original choice. Wright's perspicacity is proven by the initial impression of the clinic from the street. The textures and tonalities of the brick, Cherokee red concrete walkway, and mahogany fascia, painted an earthy red, engender a warm, welcoming feeling that continues inside.

The clinic's largest and most spectacular room is the reception and waiting area. Whereas the exterior of the building is made to hug the ground, the waiting room opens up to a sixteen-foot-high ceiling whose lift is accentuated by bands of clerestory windows with abstract sawn-wood patterns that collect the natural light. While ensuring that the waiting room accommodates the clinic's necessary functions, Wright treated it as a domestic living space. The brick fireplace serves as the nexus for an intimate seating area within close hearing and viewing distance of the reception desk. The sofas are actually composed of individual units that can be detached, rearranged, and hooked back together, and the hassocks can be easily moved next to one of the tables or alongside one of the sofas.

As clients await their appointments, they can enjoy the visual and physical comforts of the interior, including a view out the windows that wrap around the northeast corner of the reception room. Or they can walk through the back doors onto the walled terrace at the north side of the building. The triangular terrace reaches into the shaded, overgrown landscape and toward the small creek that nurtures it.

▲ Panes of glass fill the spaces between the front door and the adjacent wall of raked brick and sawn-wood windows. From both the exterior (above right) and the interior (above left), the doorway seems to float.

# FAWCETT RESIDENCE

## 1955 • Los Banos

A hundred miles inland from the Pacific Ocean, the coastal mountains of California taper off into the great Central Valley. Quilted with farms and ranches, the flat, sea-level terrain is quite distinct from the hills and ridges of Los Angeles and the Bay Area, where Wright had built his residences thus far in the state. Randall and Harriet Fawcett approached Wright to design a house within the several thousand acres of the Fawcett family farm. The valley initially struck Wright as a barren landscape to which he thought one would need to bring beauty, but he soon saw its unique perspective on the distant mountains and understood the productivity of its farmland. "I, too, have milked cows," he said to the Fawcetts, holding out one hand to look at his palm—and accepting the commission.

Wright's sympathy with the land, evident throughout the house, is particularly apparent within the large living room, the central space, from which two wings spread out at a 120-degree angle to surround terraces, a garden, and a pool. From the living room, the view to the south not only frames the garden immediately outside but reaches beyond it to encompass the broad expanse of russet fields vanishing into the horizon. Having realized that the land was much less flat than it first seemed, Wright sited the house on a long, gradual, north-to-south rise so that, from the interior, the horizon slices across the middle of the living-room windows, rooting the house ever closer to the soil. For practical reasons, the clients asked Wright to color the concrete floor a subdued clay color rather than his usual Cherokee red. He obliged—and the result unites the terraces and floor with the tones of the surrounding landscape.

▲ Fawcett residence, viewed from the north. The main entrance is in the center, under the roof overhang. To its left is the concrete-block core of the large living-room fireplace. The bedroom wing angles off to the right.

▶ Both wings of the house flow from the large living room just inside the main entry, to the left. Sawn-wood windows and clerestories bring natural light to the built-in seating next to the fireplace. The walk-in fireplace, with its battered wall and corbeled opening, is a commanding presence that is perfectly scaled in relation to the size of the space and the view out the opposite wall of glass.

▲ As well as patterning the terraces with light, openings in the roof overhangs outline views of the sky and trees. Fabrication of the copper fascia required meticulous attention to the mitered angles. The copper has patinated little in thirty years due to the dry climate and the absence of moist, salty air.

As in all of Wright's houses based on the sixty-degree triangular unit system, the Fawcett residence leads one fluidly around the interior, aided by the unifying use of Philippine mahogany in combination with the warm, sandy color of the concrete blocks. At the south side of the living room, along the glass wall that fronts the terrace, the ceiling is lowered to ease the transition to the kitchen and dining room, to the east, and to the bedrooms, to the west. The bedrooms for the Fawcetts' children are set side by side, one pair for the girls, another for the boys, each pair sharing a bathroom. At the end of the bedroom wing, at the most private spot in the house, is the master bedroom, which terminates in walls that meet at a sixty-degree angle and is sunk three feet into the ground.

Though Wright designed the Fawcett house in 1955, construction did not begin until late 1959, the year Wright died. Robert Beharka, who had apprenticed with Wright at Taliesin West, came to Los Banos to oversee the building of the house and helped make some minor changes to the plan, such as adding a door between the kitchen and the living room and moving the pool from outside the southeast wing to inside the garden. Wright's design, which included numerous built-in cabinets and pieces of furniture, was meticulously carried out. After the house was completed, the owners landscaped the grounds by creating beds and choosing plantings that harmonized with Wright's vision.

▲ The wall of windows and double doors along the south side of the living room faces onto the garden. Openings in the roof overhang—diamond shapes consistent with the sixty-degree triangular unit system—lighten the roof plane and pattern the terrace with sunlight. In the winter, the low angle of the sun pushes the islands of light and warmth onto the living-room floor.

▲ The slope of the property, rising toward the distant mountains, pulls the house close to the earth. Here, as in his other buildings, Wright used many elements—prominently raked masonry, deep roof overhangs, and ornamented fascia—to emphasize horizontality.

▶ Juxtaposing solidity and transparency at the main entry, Wright floats a nearly four-foot-wide glass door within a wall of glass that abuts the concrete-block walls. To the left are the sawn-wood windows on the living-room wall above the built-in seating next to the fireplace. The pattern of the copper-clad fascia plays off the battered walls and other angles on the exterior.

# WALTON RESIDENCE

### 1957 • Modesto

A long-time familiarity with Wright's work in the Midwest and a desire for a distinctively practical space for their family led Robert and Mary Walton to commission Wright to design their house in the Central Valley community of Modesto. Their twelve-acre site, which is typical of the valley landscape, is largely flat with subtle rises. Wright oriented the elongated L-shaped house on a north-south axis along one of these rises, far enough into the property to ensure privacy from the road.

Wright's plan for the thirty-five-hundred-square-foot house and his treatment of the materials and fenestration address the region's climate, which can be especially hot in the summer. The warm, sandy color of the concrete blocks reflects the heat of the sun and looks visually refreshing against the trees that have matured since the house was built. Contained side by side within the longest arm of the plan are four bedrooms and a playroom, all of which have floor-to-ceiling glass doors that open onto a terrace shaded by the roof overhang. As at other Usonian residences, along the primary public approach, the rows of windows below the soffit are high enough to prevent a view into the house. Here, these windows are placed on the west side to let afternoon light into the over sixty-foot-long corridor that accesses the bedrooms. When these windows and all the bedroom doors are open, nature's air-conditioning can cool and ventilate the interior. The master bedroom, which occupies the short leg of the L plan, has a similar alignment of windows and exterior doors, and its own fireplace.

▼ Walton residence, viewed from the west. The main entrance is to the north, at the end of an over sixty-foot-long walkway that begins at the carport. Jutting above the low roof of the bedroom wing is the masonry core that contains the fireplace.

▲ Walton residence, viewed from the east. The long, low, bedroom wing looks out on the swimming pool, which was added several years after the house was completed. The L shape of the pool echoes the plan of the house.

◄ Like many of Wright's dining-room tables, this one consists of modules that can be used separately or as a whole. Both the table and the straight-backed chairs are mahogany. The kitchen is through the door to the right. The windows in the left wall, above built-in cabinets, and the doors in the distance look east and south toward the swimming pool.

◄ The tall, straight-backed chairs hark back to the designs Wright pioneered earlier in the century. The difference is in the geometric detailing on their sides, formed by extending the surfaces of the arms and seats.

▲ A rhythm of geometric shapes, in mahogany, and their shadows trims the fascia. From afar, the fascia detailing both emphasizes the horizontality of the long, low, one-story house and grounds it to its site.

Where the two bedroom wings meet, a large combined dining and living area anchors the house. This space, an L shape like the overall plan, wraps around the masonry core and fireplace and the kitchen/workspace. While the sandy tonality of the blocks cools the exterior, in the interior it has a warming effect when used with Wright's customary Cherokee red concrete floor, which is scored, of course, with the unit system of the house, a thirty-two-inch square. Doors in the south wall of the dining room open onto the swimming-pool terrace, and the living room has its own terrace on the cool, north side of the house.

Wright designed mahogany furniture for all the rooms, including bunk beds for the smaller bedrooms. Throughout the house, shelves angle into corners, cabinets line walls, and small built-in tables fill niches. In the living and dining area, all the pieces of furniture, with the exception of a freestanding sofa and the lamps, are Wright's. The horizontal and vertical lines and planes of the door and window frames harmonize with those of the built-in shelves, cabinets, and bench seating, and, in turn, with those of the chairs, tables, and ottomans. The furniture is proportioned and situated to promote comfortable interaction and, when people are absent, to inhabit the room with its own distinctive presence.

# MARIN COUNTY CIVIC CENTER

### 1 9 5 7 • S a n   R a f a e l

At age ninety, Frank Lloyd Wright accepted his first and only governmental commission, an ambitious new civic center for Marin County, to be located in San Rafael, north of San Francisco. He began work in mid-1957 with a tour of the nearly 150 acres set aside for the complex. Approaching this project as he had many others throughout his career, he immediately knew he would preserve the salient features of the site—in this case, the gently rolling hills—and make them essential to his design for the main structure of the complex. The hills became the anchors for two long wings whose low, wide, ground-level arches span the landscape. One, the Administration Building, the other, the Hall of Justice, they come together at an eighty-foot-diameter dome over the county library.

The most striking aspect of Wright's design for the centerpiece of the project is its exuberance and playfulness, qualities rarely found in civic buildings. Ornament, Wright believed, should be integral to a building, "the abstract pattern of structure itself." As if seeking to create the apotheosis of this philosophy, Wright celebrates roundness—circles, spheres, semicircles, and their many structural and decorative combinations—throughout the building and on many scales. On the exterior, changes in the relative proportion of the arches and openings from level to level create a satisfying visual rhythm that is echoed in the relief patterns on the roof. On the interior, each level is a long mall with offices on either side and a central well open to the other floors. Because the offices needed a flexible layout, Wright designed a system of walls and partitions that could later be rearranged to suit the occupants.

▶ An energetic rhythm of spheres and semicircles, solids and voids, is created where the upper floor of the Administration Building meets the domed roof of the library. The large circular openings in the balcony wall and the semicircular cutouts in the roof overhangs enclose views of the landscape and sky.

▼ View of the Marin County Civic Center from the west, showing the Hall of Justice on the left, the Administration Building on the right, and the domed roof of the library in the center.

▲ Entry to the Administration Building is under the ground-level arch and through a five-part, anodized aluminum gate. The curvilinear design is accented with small gold spheres and panels in Wright's favorite red. The escalator rises to the first level.

▲ The opening through each level is wider than the one below, which makes the building appear to soar upward. At the north end of the upper floor of the Administration Building is the entrance to the library, whose curved wall of windows looks out onto the central atrium. The interior fascia, in gold anodized aluminum, repeats the exterior motif of spheres and semicircles.

Wright wanted the steel-reinforced, precast concrete structure to be compatible with its surroundings in color as well as in orientation and siting. For the walls he chose a warm sandy beige, and for the roof a gold that would blend into the burnished hillsides. Because the gold finish available at the time would not hold its intensity when used on an exterior surface, a brilliant blue was selected as an appropriate alternative. Rather than merge with the hills, it blends into the sky. Though gold was unsuitable for the roof, it is employed extensively, as on the anodized aluminum fascia. Wright's favored Cherokee red appears on the interior floors and outdoor terraces and on such anodized aluminum details as the office wall panels.

The ornamental details not only are integral to the civic center but give it a strong identity, even at a distance. From the main thoroughfares that lead toward the center and pass under the ground-level archways, it is impossible to see the entire building because the two wings meet at the domed library at a 120-degree angle. It is always possible, however, to see a detail, whether the top of the spire, or an expanse of bright blue roof, or a grouping of arches. Given the length and size of the building—it stretches for nearly one-quarter mile and at its highest is four stories—Wright's treatment of details humanizes its massiveness.

Before his death on April 9, 1959, Wright had finished the drawings for the building and the master plan for the rest of the civic center. Aaron Green, who had been involved from the beginning of the project as associate architect, and Wesley Peters, along with Taliesin Associated Architects, completed the main building in stages, beginning with the administration wing. Also part of Wright's master plan was the post office, shown here. A number of other structures were not constructed according to his design or were never built, including an innovative county fair pavilion and an amphitheater. Nevertheless, the buildings that were completed realize Wright's hope that a civic center could be "noble and inspiring."

▼ Wright brought the outside indoors by allowing for extensive plantings that grow from one floor to the next, through the wells in the office malls, and reach for the sky. Never fond of air-conditioning, he considered leaving the twenty-foot-wide upper level open to provide natural circulation of air. The final solution, made after his death, was to cover the atrium with a skylight.

▶ The spire rises 172 feet from its base at one corner of the garden terrace, its vertical momentum enhanced by the slightly angled arrangement of decorative elements. The tower is not only ornamental: it serves as a smokestack and as housing for communication equipment.

◄ Detail of tower ornament.

▼ Extending from the cafeteria on the second level of the Hall of Justice—which meets the third level of the Administration Building—the garden terrace projects northeast in Wright's typical ship's-prow shape. The terrace offers a view of the distant hills and of the entire 880-foot length of the Hall of Justice to the northwest.

▼ Designed by Wright as part of his original master plan for the civic center, the elliptical, concrete-block post office was completed before the main building across from it. The cantilevered portico seems to slice through the front wall, and its fascia reiterates in relief the fascia detailing used in the main building. This is Wright's only completed commission for the federal government.

▶ The domed roof of the library shades the terrace on the level below, which surrounds the board of supervisors' offices and meeting rooms. The vertical members, which are non–load bearing, are treated as two offset elements: one a concrete plinth that rises from the terrace, the other a gold anodized aluminum taper that drops from the soffit to meet it.

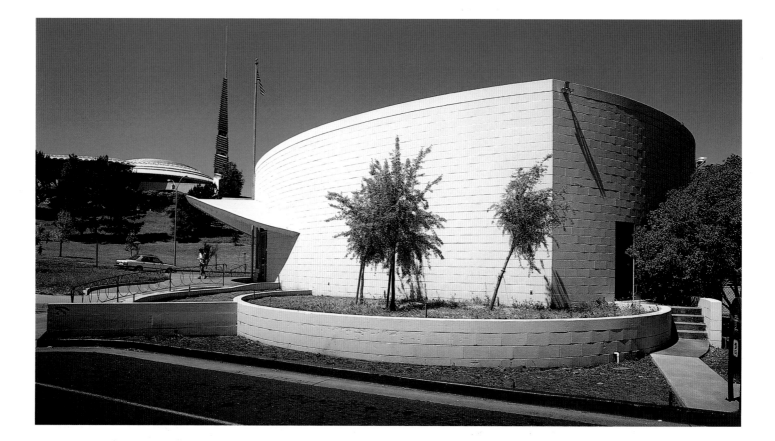

# ABLIN RESIDENCE

## 1958 • Bakersfield

▲ Included as part of Wright's original design, the gate was fabricated later, according to his specifications, of steel painted black and Cherokee red. The adjacent sculpture of Cor-ten steel is by artist Gene Flores, an admirer of the architect's work, who incorporated the triangular module used throughout the house. A smaller gate in a similar design leads from the main entry to the pool and its surrounding terrace.

**W**right's gate of Cherokee red panels held by lines of black-painted steel makes an appropriate greeting across the driveway that rises up to the residence of Dr. George and Millie Ablin. Standing out against the green landscape of this area of suburban Bakersfield, it announces the geometric theme that one will encounter at the house itself. Next to the gate, as a homage to Wright's composition, is a black steel sculpture by a contemporary admirer of the architect's work. The friendly juxtaposition reveals the Ablins' artistic interests, one of their motivations for asking Wright to design a house that would combine their aesthetic leanings with their need for a practical living space.

Having already designed two houses for the Central Valley, the Fawcett and the Walton, Wright was familiar with the terrain and climate of the region. Though differing in plan from the Fawcett house, the Ablin also has two wings surrounding an exterior area that extends the interior living spaces onto terraces, lawn, and a swimming pool. As at so many of Wright's California houses, the sloping roof planes ground the residence to the coolness of the landscaped site and shade the walls, walkways, and terraces. Wright chose an especially warm palette that suits the location and facilitates the transition from indoors to outdoors. The earthy Cherokee red of the concrete terraces and walkways leads to the pink of the concrete-block walls, which appear subtle or vibrant depending upon the intensity of the light.

Prominently visible from the main approach to the house, the anchoring masonry core containing the kitchen impresses one with its angled walls

◄ Walls of perforated blocks filled with clear plexiglass give the Ablin kitchen much more natural light than is found in many of Wright's Usonian workspaces. The hexagonal stools were designed by Wright for use with the counter to turn it into an eating area.

▲ Ablin residence, viewed from the southeast. The two bedroom wings meet at the large living area, which looks onto an expanse of lawn.

composed entirely of plexiglass-filled concrete blocks. The arrowlike pattern was one Wright had used before, in the 1950 Palmer house in Michigan. The perforated blocks visually lighten the four walls that project into the terrace, which surrounds the west side of the house. More impressive yet is the effect inside the kitchen, where the perforated block walls are like screens of light.

As in all of Wright's Usonian designs, the living space is the center of the plan and is arranged to be the locus of human activity. From the fireplace within the concrete-block core, the space soars upward and outward, culminating in two walls that frame the landscape and sky. Intimate areas are tucked at either side of the hexagonal space, within sight of the fireplace. One is a wall of built-in seating and shelves below the low ceiling just inside the entry. The other is the dining area, where Wright orchestrated an elegant continuation of the wall and cabinetry into the dining room table and chairs, all in mahogany. Over the years since the house was built, the owners have had Wright's Philippine mahogany furniture completed. The armchairs, side chairs, and ottomans—upholstered in the pomegranate color he originally specified—make the Ablin living room among the most harmonious and authentic spaces found in Wright's California houses.

▲ Wright designed the parallelogram-shaped dining table in three sections, each of which can be used independently here or elsewhere in the house. One end of the table fits into the shelf that continues beyond the built-in cabinets into the corner of the space.

▶ Frosted, rather than clear, plexiglass is used in the blocks over which cabinets are mounted.

◄ A harmonious use of materials, colors, and the triangular unit system characterizes the furniture Wright designed for the Ablin house. The sawn-wood detailing in the armchair echoes the arrowlike perforation in the concrete blocks, and the small flag shapes resemble those used on the steel entry gate.

◄ The living-room ceiling rises to approximately sixteen feet at the mitered angle where the walls of glass meet and project onto the terrace. The doors and their frames, which are parallelograms, and the window mullions at once accentuate the lift of the ceiling and ground it to the rest of the room. Wright designed not only the furniture but also the easels for the display of the Ablins' art collection.

# PILGRIM CONGREGATIONAL CHURCH

## 1958 • Redding

I n the last decade of his life, Wright designed several religious buildings, including a synagogue in Pennsylvania and Unitarian and Greek Orthodox churches in Wisconsin. Another was the Pilgrim Congregational Church in Redding, California. When the congregation's building committee contacted him through Taliesin West in 1957, Wright responded enthusiastically. "Tell the people of the little church," he answered, "that I will help them out." He was unable to visit the site: just under five acres on a hilltop in the northern Central Valley with views of the snow-capped mountains of the southern Cascade Range. For details on the topography and surroundings, he relied on the assistance of several of his associates and on a survey and drawings sent to him by the congregation, which were so detailed that they specified the precise location of every tree, sizable rock, and other natural landmark on the property.

What Wright ultimately designed was not a "little church" but an ambitious building in a style the architect whimsically called "pole-and-boulder gothic." The plan, employing a triangular module, incorporated four wings: a one-hundred-seat chapel, a three-hundred-seat sanctuary, offices and a fellowship hall, and classrooms. Above the sanctuary narthex in the plan is a five-level tower culminating in a spire. Wright took full advantage of the contours and distinctive features of the site by placing the amphitheater requested by the congregation just below the sanctuary and near a stream. Hampered by lack of funds, however, by 1963 the congregation had completed only the fellowship hall, the classrooms, and part of the office wing.

▲ Pilgrim Congregational Church, viewed from the northeast.

▶ The triangular floor plan, the orientation of the concrete beams, and the arrangement of the altar give the fellowship hall a satisfying asymmetricality. Cutouts in the concrete beams along the right side of the hall accommodate the roof rafters. The soffit, with its decorative notches, and the ceiling are cedar. Added in the late 1970s, the stained-glass windows were originally clerestories. Through the door at the left is the classroom wing.

◀ The entrance to the church is six
steps below the front terrace. To the
left is the fellowship hall; to the right,
the offices.

Despite these and other modifications—including the addition of a basement—the finished portion retains the spirit of Wright's vision of the fellowship hall as resembling the form of a tent, an ancient and archetypal human shelter. The concrete supports pierce the peaked metal roof of the "tent" and seem to lift it upward. In contrast, the siting and the rockwork make the building "belong to the ground," as Wright once described this essential aspect of his philosophy. As in many Usonian residences, a masonry core contains a fireplace, and the sixty-degree triangular module is expressed in the diamonds scored on the polished concrete floor. The classroom wing at the southeast of the hall is a series of parallelogram-shaped rooms conforming to the unit system of the plan and terminating in a triangular room. At the northeast side of the wing, masonry walls define a triangular sunken garden.

Members of the congregation participated significantly in the building of the church, even collecting from wide-ranging locations the many tons of rock needed for the stonework. Aaron Green of Wright's San Francisco office and Tony Puttnam and John Rattenbury, both of Taliesin West, assisted at various stages from review of the site to supervision of the construction, which took place after Wright's death. The congregation hopes someday to realize the architect's entire design. Then it will be possible to appreciate how Wright oriented the building—so that its north face would offer an inspirational view of snow-covered Mount Shasta.

▲ The pulpit is built into the steps of
the altar. It and the communion table,
bench seat, and planter are made of
straight-grain Douglas fir. The tabletop
is cherry veneer.

# BELL-FELDMAN RESIDENCE

### 1974 • Berkeley

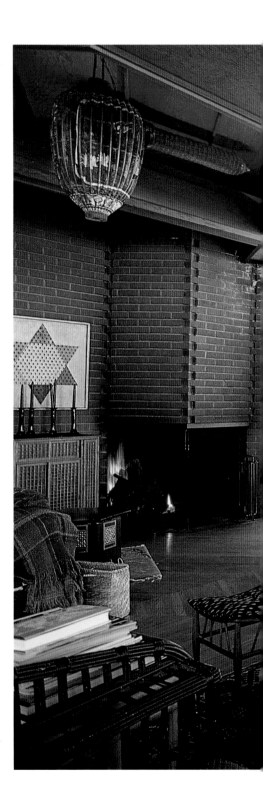

As many of Wright's commissions that were realized, there were even more commissions that were never built. In California, they range from Aline Barnsdall's arts community of the 1920s to the 1948 Daphne Funeral Chapel, an unusual complex of chapels and gardens in San Francisco, to the 1949 proposal for a bridge over San Francisco Bay. Another project, a 1940 residence for Lewis N. Bell in Los Angeles, remained unbuilt until 1974, when Hillary and Joe Feldman purchased the plans and constructed it in Berkeley. Wright's plans for the original client called the house "Hillcrown," an appellation that applies just as well to its current site. Although the residence is not set literally on the crown of a hill, it is sited on the sloping property so that, as at the Freeman house in Los Angeles, the living area gives the feeling of being perched high above the surroundings and amid the treetops of a well-populated but wooded residential neighborhood.

In this wood-and-brick house, the living area is prominent not only because the plan reflects Wright's Usonian concepts but also because the residence is so small. The interior includes two small hexagonal bedrooms placed side by side at the east end of the house with a bathroom in between them. Projecting from these two hexagons is the large hexagon of the living area, in the center of which is the masonry core, an even smaller hexagon, containing the kitchen and fireplace. Three walls are composed of floor-to-ceiling glass doors and horizontally paned windows that expand the living room out beyond the trees toward a panorama of San Francisco Bay.

▼ Feldman residence,
viewed from the northeast.
From the carport, to the left,
the house reaches west to the
terrace outside the living
room, at the far right.

◄ Three sides of the
hexagonal living room are
glass walls that look out on a
terrace and garden. The
clerestory-filled center of the
ceiling and the spiraled
molding restate, on different
scales, the hexagons of the
overall plan. Various woods
are used on the interior:
Douglas fir on the ceiling,
redwood for some of the
walls and detailing, and oak
for the finish flooring.

The double doors, located at a 120-degree angle where the walls meet, dissolve the walls when they are opened onto the terrace.

The detailing is similar to that of Wright's other houses of the 1940s. The brick walls are horizontally raked, and the flat roof plane appears to float over the clerestories, which are sawn wood. The Cherokee red concrete terrace extends two feet inside the glass walls of the living room to meet the finish flooring, which is oak. The triangular ceiling lights are recessed to avoid protruding into the flowing space. And the most unusual detail is the molding on the living-room ceiling: an angular spiral within each segment of the hexagon, which abstractly recalls the chambers of a shell, an architectural construction of nature, one of Wright's great sources of inspiration.

◀ The doors from the living room to the terrace are located where the glass walls meet at a 120-degree angle. Opening the doors dissolves the corners and eliminates the boundary between indoors and outdoors.

▶ Sawn-wood patterns like those in the clerestories embellish the screen that closes off the kitchen from the living room.

# FURTHER READING

The following selection of books includes those that are devoted to Wright's work in California and those, like the architect's autobiography, that discuss his California buildings in the context of his entire career.

Futagawa, Yukio, and Bruce Brooks Pfeiffer. *Frank Lloyd Wright, Monographs, Studies, and Renderings.* Vols. 1-12. Tokyo: ADA Edita, Tokyo Company, 1988.

———. *Frank Lloyd Wright, Selected Houses.* Vols. 6-8. Tokyo: ADA Edita, Tokyo Company, 1990–.

Gebhard, David, and Scot Zimmerman. *Romanza: The California Architecture of Frank Lloyd Wright.* San Francisco: Chronicle Books, 1988.

Green, Aaron G. *An Architecture for Democracy: Frank Lloyd Wright, The Marin County Civic Center, A Narrative.* San Francisco: Grendon, 1990.

Hanks, David A. *The Decorative Designs of Frank Lloyd Wright.* New York: E. P. Dutton, 1979.

Hanna, Paul R., and Jean S. Hanna. *Frank Lloyd Wright's Hanna House, The Clients' Report.* Carbondale, Ill.: Southern Illinois University Press, 1981.

Hildebrand, Grant. *The Wright Space, Pattern & Meaning in Frank Lloyd Wright's Houses.* Seattle: University of Washington Press, 1991.

Hoffmann, Donald. *Frank Lloyd Wright's Hollyhock House.* New York: Dover Publications, 1992.

Lind, Carla. *The Wright Style.* New York: An Archetype Press Book, Simon & Schuster, 1992.

Pfeiffer, Bruce Brooks, ed. *Frank Lloyd Wright: Letters to Clients.* Fresno, Calif.: The Press at California State University, 1982.

———. *Frank Lloyd Wright in the Realm of Ideas.* Carbondale, Ill.: Southern Illinois University Press, 1988.

Secrest, Meryle. *Frank Lloyd Wright.* New York: Alfred A. Knopf, 1992.

Sergeant, John. *Frank Lloyd Wright's Usonian Houses: The Case for Organic Architecture.* New York: Whitney Library of Design, 1976; Watson-Guptill Publications, 1984.

Smith, Kathryn. *Hollyhock House and Olive Hill, Buildings and Projects for Aline Barnsdall.* New York: Rizzoli International Publications, 1992.

Sweeney, Robert L. *Wright in Hollywood, Visions of a New Architecture,* Cambridge, Mass.: MIT Press, 1993.

Wright, Frank Lloyd. *An Autobiography.* Reprint. New York: Horizon Press, 1977.

———. *The Natural House.* New York: Horizon Press, 1954.